THE MURDERED DEAD SPEAK BOOK II

The Murdered Dead Speak
Book II

Murder Never Dies

SHIRLEY SMOLKO

Cavallaro Publishing

Cover Design by Shirley Smolko

Printed in the U.S.A.

First Printing, 2024

Print ISBN: 978-1-958104-09-5

Ebook ISBN: 978-1-958104-10-1

Library of Congress Control Number: 2024910281

Cavallaro Publishing

N. Venice, FL

To Joe, my husband, and Ernest Hemingway, my writing guide: many thanks for encouraging me to write.

There was a day when I had been praying and seeking guidance from the Creator as to whether or not I should continue writing. On the night of this day, my husband dreamed he was having a cocktail with Ernest Hemingway at Sloppy Joe's. In the dream, he asked Mr. Hemingway, "Do you have any advice for my wife?" Ernest took a swig of his drink, turned his head, looked at Joe, and said, "Tell Shirl to keep at it."

The next morning, we woke up facing each other in bed. Joe looked me directly in the eyes and said, "I have a message from Ernest Hemingway; he said for you to keep at it." Now, this wouldn't normally have been a big deal for me; however, because my husband didn't know I had prayed the day before for guidance as to whether or not I should continue writing, it was definitely a big deal. It was a concrete answer to prayer. So, once again, here I go. I'm gonna keep at it!

CONTENTS

~ 1 ~

MURDER NEVER DIES

Introduction

Step into the astral realm, where the veil between the living and the dead is lifted, as I open portals to the past and engage in chilling conversations with the spirits of infamous murder victims. *In The Murdered Dead Speak Book II: Murder Never Dies*, I communicate with the souls of Maria Marten, Helen Jewett, Mary Cecilia Rogers, Blas Trujillo, and Julia Wallace.

These spirits share the intimate details of their long-buried cases, shedding light on the unsolved mysteries surrounding their tragic deaths while revealing startling insights into the minds of their murderers. The book captures the voices of the departed as they recount the events leading up to their fateful ends, the chilling moments of their demise, and the lingering questions that have haunted investigators for generations.

From the haunting love story and betrayal of Maria Marten to the tragic death of a New York high-class prostitute Helen Jewett, the enigmatic circumstances of Mary Cecilia Rogers' demise, the gruesome fate of Blas Trujillo, and the mysterious death of Julia Wallace, each story unfolds like a spectral tapestry woven with threads of sorrow, betrayal, and unanswered questions. Through my connection with the spirit world, you will witness the unveiling of long-buried secrets as the victims themselves recount the chilling details of their murders.

Before writing book I of *The Murdered Dead Speak*, Blas Trujillo came to me in a dream asking that I tell his story. Although his story did not make it into Book I, I promised to include it in Book II; however, I needed more stories to create a book. So I scanned a list of unsolved murder victims to determine their willingness to tell their stories. I called upon the spirits on the list and asked, "*If you can hear me and seek resolution, I invite you to speak through me. Share your stories and let the truth rise from the shadows..*" Four out of twenty spirits on this list came forward. These souls were: Maria Marten, Helen Jewett, Mary Cecilia Rogers, and Julia Wallace.

As soon as I sent out the invitation, the atmosphere seemed to shift as the spirits responded, their energies intertwining with my own, creating a conduit for the spirit communication to come in which they would reveal the intricacies of their fates and the identities of those who had condemned them to a state of unrest. It was then that I knew they wanted to tell their story through me.

Before beginning each chapter, I sat in my favorite comfy chair with my MacBook Air on my lap, closed my eyes, took a deep breath, and asked the spirit that I was writing about to come into my space. Almost immediately, I would have a chill pass through my body as the spirit I summoned stepped into my presence and began communicating their story to me, mainly through the psychic faculties of clairvoyance, clairaudience, and clairsentience.

In the chapters that follow, prepare to embark on a journey into the past, guided by the spirits of the murdered dead. Together, the spirits and I will unveil the mysteries that have perplexed investigators, historians, and true crime enthusiasts for generations.

In chapter two, the quiet village of Polstead echoes an unsolved mystery that continues to linger like a haunting melody. The year was 1827, and the tale of Maria Marten and the notorious Red Barn had become a chilling refrain etched into the annals of true crime history.

Maria Marten, a young and radiant woman, left the safety of her humble home on a sunny day in May to meet her lover, William Corder, within the shadowy embrace of the Red Barn. Although it no longer stands, the very mention of this crimson-hued structure still sends shivers down the spines of the villagers, for it was within these walls that the course of Maria's destiny would be forever altered.

With dreams in her eyes and love in her heart, Maria had fallen under the spell of William Corder. Yet, unbeknownst to her, the man she trusted harbored secrets darker than the night itself. The disappearance of Maria Marten sent shockwaves through Polstead, and as whispers of foul play spread like wildfire, the specter of suspicion fell upon William Corder. An investigation ensued, unearthing a tale of betrayal, deceit, and a love turned lethal. Guided by Maria Marten, I reveal the untold details of that ill-fated day, thereby verifying the identity of the one who condemned her to the restless shadows. As we delve into the spiritual realm, the truth will rise like a ghostly mist, bringing justice to a soul long denied its peace.

In the third chapter, the tale of Helen Jewett unfolds like a tragic sonnet of lust, betrayal, and untimely demise. The year was 1836, and the bustling metropolis was a melting pot of dreams and despair, where the promise of opportunity clashed with the harsh realities of life and the dimly lit corridors of New York City were aglow with gas lamps that cast their eerie shadows on cobblestone streets,

Helen Jewett, a young and captivating woman, found herself ensnared in the tangled web of the city's notorious brothels—a world where desire and desperation collided in a dance of forbidden pleasures. Her beauty was renowned, her charm irresistible, and within the walls of the elegant brothel on Thomas Street, she reigned as queen of the demimonde.

But beneath the gilded facade of her glamorous existence, the specter of violence loomed on the horizon. On a cold April night, the silence of the brothel was shattered by a savage attack that left Helen Jewett lifeless, her body consumed by flames. The murder sent shockwaves through the city, igniting a firestorm of scandal and intrigue that would captivate the public imagination for decades to come.

As investigators delved into the sordid world of the brothel, the spotlight fell on Richard P. Robinson, a prominent client of Helen's and a man with a penchant for jealousy and possessiveness. Yet, despite mounting evidence pointing to his guilt, the case remained shrouded in ambiguity, leaving the truth obscured by the mists of uncertainty.

In the fourth chapter, the disappearance of Mary Cecilia Rogers —the beautiful cigar girl—casts a mysterious shadow over the city that never sleeps. The year was 1841, and 19th-century New York City, where gas lamps flickered in the evening glow and horse-drawn carriages clattered along cobblestone lanes, pulsated with life yet harbored many secrets. Her story unfolds against the backdrop of a small tobacco shop nestled in the neighborhood of SoHo, where she worked as a clerk. Mary's fate took a dark turn on a summer day that would become etched in the annals of the city's history. The sudden and unexplained disappearance of the beautiful cigar girl sent shockwaves through the community, and the streets of Manhattan became a stage for a mystery that would baffle investigators and captivate the public imagination.

Her lifeless body surfaced in the waters of the Hudson River. The city, gripped by speculation and fueled by sensationalist media, clamored for answers. The questions surrounding Mary's demise echoed through the avenues and alleyways, but the truth remained elusive, obscured by the fog of uncertainty.

As I opened the channel of communication with the spirit of Mary, the spectral curtain rose, revealing her untold story and the identity of her murderers who consigned her to the astral shadows. The streets of old Manhattan await, echoing with the whispers of a maiden lost in time, yearning to share the secrets that have bound her spirit for far too long.

In Chapter Five, my husband and I had planned a day trip to Ybor City in Tampa, FL., to do some touring and take in the essence of this exciting little Latin City within a city. This trip occurred in August, ironically, Mr. Trujillo died in August. A few days before embarking on our trip, I had a dream one night in which I was transported to another time and place to witness the life and murder of a very kind and successful cigar manufacturer whose death had been misclassified as a suicide.

The year was 1900, and the multicultural enclave of Ybor City in Tampa, Florida, was a melting pot of diverse cultures and aspirations. The aromatic scent of tobacco smoke hung thick in the humid air as the respected manufacturer of fine cigars revealed the detailed events leading up to his untimely death. The day after my dream, research for our planned trip put a name to the kindly man —Blas Trujillo.

As I sat down to write this chapter, the spirit of Blas emerged from the astral shadows, eagerly waiting for me to share my dream of the events leading up to his murder, ensuring that I got the story right. I could feel Mr. Trujillo's spirit and hear him gently encouraging me as I wrote. His is the voice of a gentle and loving soul. Only a hideous monster could kill this sweet man!

In the sixth and last chapter, a chilling story of murder emerges that etched Julia Wallace into the annals of unsolved crime mysteries. The year was 1931, and the suburbs of Anfield would soon become the stage for a dreadful performance that left detectives perplexed and the community in a state of shock.

Julia Wallace, a reserved and unassuming woman, was the victim of a brutal murder. Her husband, William Herbert Wallace, an insurance agent with a penchant for chess, became entangled in a web of suspicion when a seemingly innocent evening turned into a sinister plot that would leave Julia lifeless in their home on Wolverton Street.

The saga began with a cryptic telephone call, summoning William to a fictitious address on the pretext of a new insurance policy. Little did he know that this call would set in motion a sequence of events that would lead to the murder of his wife and propel the Wallace case into the realm of the inexplicable.

As William arrived at the designated address, he discovered it was a mere mirage—a cruel ruse intended to divert him from his home. Racing back to Wolverton Street, he was met with a gruesome scene. Julia lay lifeless, the victim of a brutal attack.

Was William Wallace the mastermind orchestrating an elaborate plan, or was he an unwitting pawn in a larger scheme? These two questions have lingered like ghosts in the corridors of justice, haunting the city of Liverpool and leaving the fate of Julia Wallace shrouded in mystery.

In this chapter, we step into the astral realm, where Julia Wallace herself awaits. As I open the channel to the spirit world, Julia's voice emerges from the shadows, ready to share the untold story of that fateful night.

The Murdered Dead Speak II: Murder Never Dies is a captivating journey into the unknown, blending true crime narratives with the supernatural and offering readers a glimpse into the shadows of the past. As I bridge the gap between this world and the next, the spirits speak, seeking justice, closure, and a chance to rest in peace finally. Will the revelations the spirits provide be the key to solving these age-old mysteries, or will they only deepen the enigma surrounding these notorious cases? Prepare to be enthralled, as the spirits speak.

~ 2 ~

CASE FILE #1: MARIA MARTEN-THE RED BARN MURDER

Maria Marten
Public Domain

Case Summary

Name of Deceased: Maria Marten

Date of Birth: July 24, 1801

Date of Death: May 18, 1827

Location: The Red Barn, Polstead, Suffolk, England

Deceased Found by: Thomas Marten

Relationship to the Deceased: Father

Complainant: Thomas Marten

Relationship to the Deceased: Father

Witness #1: Stepmother, Ann Marten, had several dreams about Maria's grave in the red barn.

Witness #2: Maria's brother, George Martin, saw Corder crossing a field, carrying a pick-ax across his shoulder on the day he had supposedly left with Maria to get married.

Estimated Time of Death: Sometime after half-past noon on the day she left home. She was never seen again that day but Corder was.

Weapons discovered: Pistols in a black silk bag that had belonged to Maria.

Positions of Body: Buried in a shallow grave of about two feet. Her body was placed head first in a sack so small that she had to be curled up into a fetal position to fit in it.

Wounds: Deep lacerations to the right neck, right face, and left chest; pistol ball wound through the left cheek with a trajectory through the right eye.

Blood Splatters: None

Autopsy Findings #1: See below

Autopsy Findings #2: See below

Disposition: Closed Case

Convicted Murderer: William (Bill) Corder

Un-convicted Murderer: The evil spirit possessing William Corder

Background Informant Sources:

Text #1: Curtis, J. (1828). *An Authentic and Faithful History of the Mysterious Murder of Maria Marten*, Thomas Kelly.

Text #2: An Accurate Account of the Trial of William Corder for the Murder of Maria Marten. (1828). George Foster.

Background on the Murder of Maria Marten

Maria Marten was blessed with a remarkable memory and a strong desire to gain valuable knowledge. It's reasonable to believe that with proper education, she could have become a highly accomplished woman. One particular aspect of her character that garners sympathy for her tragic fate is her deep filial piety. She always spoke of her late mother with sorrow, and undoubtedly, the lessons imparted by her kind-hearted mother in her early years played a significant role in shaping her behavior during her youth. The bond between Maria and her father was also extraordinary.

It would have been ideal if Maria had not let go of her early values and principles as she matured. Up until she turned seventeen, Maria Marten lived contentedly in a modest cottage, setting an example of domestic excellence that even older women admired. Unfortunately, we must now introduce a darker element into the story.

Maria possessed exceptional physical beauty, with an attractive face, a graceful figure, and an elegant demeanor that reflected her innocence and purity. Given these qualities, it's not surprising that she attracted admirers. Considering the realities of human nature, it's also understandable that she, an inexperienced and guileless young woman, succumbed to flattery and chose an unworthy object of affection without careful consideration.

Tragically, this became her fate. At the age of eighteen, the once-happy and virtuous Maria succumbed to the persuasion of a deceitful individual and fell victim to his greed, losing her most precious possession—her virtue. This loss was keenly felt by someone with her character. From that moment, instead of innocence and contentment, guilt and shame became her constant companions. The beginning of her descent into sin was like the breaking of a dam, and once the line between virtue and vice was crossed, the ensuing cascade of evils was impossible to predict.

There have been numerous reports about who initially seduced the country girl, Maria, prompting us to investigate and gather information from reliable sources. Thomas Corder, the brother of William, the prisoner, was drawn to Maria's striking beauty. He often visited her cottage, which he had to pass daily because part of his father's land was in that direction. It's worth noting that Maria, dedicated to her domestic responsibilities, led a somewhat secluded life and did not engage in the common practice of girls her age and background, which involved going for walks. This pattern continued even up to the time of her death.

It's said that Mr. Corder made respectable advances towards Maria. As the son of a wealthy farmer and a reasonably presentable young man, it would not have been surprising for a girl of her age and circumstances to accept his sincere declarations of love. A close relationship developed as a result of these advances, but it seems that Thomas Corder wished to keep it a secret, possibly due to the economic disparity between them. Regardless, they maintained regular correspondence, and what Maria believed to be an honorable courtship turned into an illicit affair, resulting in her becoming a mother.

As often happens in such situations, once her true condition was discovered, Thomas's visits became less frequent until they were almost entirely discontinued. Maria was left to lament her own imprudence and reflect on her lover's broken promises. It can be reasonably inferred that genuine love did not motivate Thomas Corder, as evidenced by his subsequent actions. Although he had every reason to believe that he had taken something precious from her (as did those who knew her), he either withheld financial support out of selfish motives or for some other reason, even though he had no intention of marrying her.

For some undisclosed reason, perhaps holding out hope that her seducer might change and fulfill his promises, the deceived young woman never sought a magistrate's order of affiliation. Instead, Corder provided her with financial assistance during her childbirth and afterward, similar to what would have been expected under such an order. Unfortunately, the illegitimate infant cared for lovingly by its young mother, passed away at a very young age and was buried in Polstead churchyard, near where its unfortunate mother would later find rest from her worldly troubles and anxieties. This aspect of the story adds another layer of complexity to an already mysterious case, involving Maria being seduced by one brother and later forming a relationship with another member of the same family. Now, let's delve into another part of Maria's tragic history.

After her relationship with Thomas Corder had completely ended, Maria developed a close friendship with a highly respectable gentleman. We won't mention his name because his conduct towards Maria was entirely honorable, in stark contrast to the individuals she had been involved with previously and later. With this gentleman, Maria had a child named Thomas Henry, a beautiful boy. Thomas Henry, who currently resides in the cottage with his grandfather, has always received generous support from his biological father. This father intends to provide him with a proper education and make future provisions for his well-being.

It's important to note Maria's sense of honor in this context. When the gentleman initially expressed interest in her, she candidly disclosed her prior relationship with Thomas Corder and her pregnancy at the time. Therefore, when their relationship progressed, he had no reason to doubt her integrity. In fact, it's possible that her grace and charm may have led him to seek her companionship.

The fact that a girl who had lost her reputation and self-esteem continued down a troubled path might not be surprising, especially when considering her lively and optimistic personality, and perhaps even a touch of ambition. As previously revealed in evidence, there were heated exchanges between William Corder and Maria concerning his secret possession of a five-pound note meant to assist her in supporting her surviving child. Corder once asked her not to mention the matter again, assuring, in the presence of her family, that as long as he had a shilling, neither she nor her child would suffer want.

Various rumors circulated about this intercepted note (there was only one), so we provided detailed information as conveyed by someone involved in the investigation. When Maria Marten did not receive a remittance from the usual source, she became concerned and wrote to the gentleman, expressing her disappointment and financial difficulties. In response, and more to clear himself of any negligence than to recover the money, he initiated an inquiry at the post office. This inquiry revealed that the exact note he had sent had passed through the hands of a person named Corder.

Following the complaint filed at her office, Miss Savage, the postmistress in Colchester, along with a solicitor, visited Corder's mother to investigate whether any family members had knowledge of the note in question and its source. It has been suggested in the public sphere that either she or William Corder changed the bill, but William had used his brother James's name to introduce an element of mystery into the transaction. However, it's important to clarify that this is not the case.

When the solicitor and postmistress arrived, William Corder was at home but claimed complete ignorance of the matter under inquiry. They summoned a neighbor who, understanding the nature of the investigation, went to the church where John Corder, the elder brother of the prisoner, was engaged in parochial duties. However, John could not shed any light on the matter.

Later, Mr. P—, the previously mentioned gentleman, visited Hadleigh Bank a few days after the incident and spoke with Mr. Baker, one of the firm members. Mr. Baker inquired about the first name of the Corder who had severe nearsightedness, and Mr. P— confirmed it was William. Mr. Baker then revealed that they had endorsed the name "James Corder" on the bill, believing it to be the younger brother's, after making inquiries. Mr. Baker, Jr. also recalled mentioning to his father how extraordinarily nearsighted the young Corder was.

The day after this conversation, the informant visited James Corder and asked him to discuss the matter with his brother William. William initially denied any knowledge of the transaction but mentioned that he planned to visit the bankers in Hadleigh to clarify matters. He did so and, at first, displayed a high-handed attitude, questioning why Mr. Baker had raised unfounded suspicions against him and claiming a mistaken identity. However, Mr. Baker, Jr. asserted his confidence that William was the person involved, to the point of being willing to swear to it if necessary. He advised William to go to Colchester promptly to resolve the matter. It appears that William followed this advice, going directly from Hadleigh to Colchester on the same evening to address the issue.

To shield himself from disgrace and the impending legal consequences of a potential prosecution, he coerced Maria into an action that she would later deeply regret. Specifically, he compelled her to lie by contradicting her previous statement and admitting that she had received the money before it was given. During the brief period between this incident and her sudden departure from Polstead (as it was initially believed), the gentleman sent his payment by endorsing half of a banknote. He insisted on receiving a handwritten acknowledgment from Maria before dispatching the other half of the note.

This infatuated young woman seemed not to have gained wisdom from her experiences and hardships. Otherwise, why would she have placed her trust in the promises of the brother of her initial seducer, especially considering she must have been aware of his character and disposition? Nevertheless, that's precisely what happened, and William Corder became the father of her third child. After giving birth, both she and her father often implored Corder to fulfill his promise and rescue her from disgrace and ruin through a legitimate marriage. However, he consistently found excuses to postpone it but never outright denied his obligation to fulfill their agreement.

There is another mysterious aspect connected to the child Maria bore, of which Corder was the father. The baby gradually became ill and died shortly before its ill-fated mother. It's worth noting that those who witnessed the child's decline believed it was due to natural causes. However, the secretive manner in which the infant's body was removed from Marten's cottage has given rise to numerous speculations and, for some, well-founded suspicions of foul play. It's quite unusual that Corder took the child away in a box, claiming he intended to have it buried in Sudbury. His sole explanation for this choice was that the infant had been born there. Since the discovery of Maria's murder, a thorough investigation has revealed beyond a doubt that the child was never given a Christian burial in Sudbury or any other legitimate cemetery near Polstead.

Events Leading up to the Murder of Maria Marten According to the Testimony of Ann Marten:

During the trial of William Corder, the first witness called was Ann Marten, the wife of Thomas Marten, who testified that she resided in Polstead, and her husband's daughter was Maria Marten. She had been acquainted with the prisoner, who lived in their neighborhood, for 17 years. The prisoner had an intimate relationship with Maria and used to visit their cottage frequently for more than a year leading up to May 18th of the previous year.

Maria became pregnant during their relationship, which occurred in Sudbury. It was approximately seven weeks before May 1827 when she returned to her father's house, accompanied by an infant child who unfortunately passed away about two weeks later. Corder continued to visit their house and openly acknowledged that he was the father of this child. He often engaged in conversations with Maria, and when the child was buried, he claimed to have taken it to Sudbury for the burial.

She recalled that he had mentioned a £5 note on several occasions, and Maria used to complain that he had taken away her means of sustenance and her child's as well. Maria had a child from a previous relationship, and this child was cared for by the witness.

Mr. Corder informed Maria that the parish authorities were planning to take legal action against her for having illegitimate children. She specifically remembered the Sunday before Friday, May 18th. On that Sunday evening, the prisoner visited their cottage, where he stayed for about half an hour to three-quarters of an hour. Afterward, he left with Maria, both of them mentioning their intention to travel to Ipswich early on the following Monday morning after spending the night at his mother's house.

Maria returned home between three and four o'clock in the morning, and Corder visited again on that day. He stated that they would postpone their journey to Ipswich to Wednesday night due to Stoke Fair. However, they did not proceed on that date as planned because he claimed his brother James was on the brink of death.

On Friday, which is the day mentioned in the indictment, around 11 or 12 o'clock, Corder arrived and went upstairs to see the witness and Maria. To Maria, he said, "I have come, Maria. Make haste. I am ready to go." She responded, "How can I leave at this time of day without anyone seeing me?" He reassured her, saying, "Don't worry. We have faced many disappointments, but this time we won't be let down."

After this conversation, she inquired, "How should I prepare myself to leave?" He answered, "You can make your way to the Red Barn and wait for me there later in the evening." Maria then asked, "How should I pack my belongings?" He assured her he would take care of it, carry her things to the barn, and return to accompany her. He added that none of his workers were in the fields or at the barn, so the path was clear. Maria's possessions, including a reticule, a wicker basket, a velvet bag, two pairs of black silk stockings, a silk gown of the same color, a cambric skirt, and other clothing items, were placed in a brown Holland bag, which Corder carried away in his hand.

Maria then dressed in a brown coat, a striped waistcoat, and blue trousers. Underneath her outer garments, she wore a petticoat, white stays, a green and red silk handkerchief, and an Irish linen chemise that she made. The witness had helped Maria fasten her stays that morning and was familiar with the marks on them, which she described, as well as the marks on the shoes Maria was wearing.

The reason they were going to Ipswich on that day, as explained by William, was that John Baalham, the constable, had approached him in the morning at the stable. Baalham had mentioned receiving a letter from Mr. Whitmore of London, which contained a warrant to apprehend Maria and prosecute her for her illegitimate children. The witness expressed her concern, saying, "Oh, William, if you had only married Maria before this child was born, as I had hoped, all of this could have been avoided." William responded, "Well, I'm heading to Ipswich to marry her tomorrow morning." The witness further inquired, "William, what will you do if that doesn't work out?" He assured her, saying, "Don't worry; she will be my lawful wife before I return, or I will find her a place to work until we can make it happen."

At around half-past noon, Maria then left, with Corder instructing the witness to keep an eye on the garden to ensure nobody saw them departing. They exited through different doors, with Maria dressed in men's clothing and wearing a hat belonging to the prisoner. She had a large comb in her hair, along with a smaller one, and was wearing earrings. Together, they headed in the direction of the Red Barn. After that day, the witness never saw either of them again, nor did she ever see Maria again.

Autopsy #1: Performed by Surgeon John Lawson

I was present on April 20th when the Coroner's jury went to view the body found in the Red Barn. The body had not been disturbed, except for the removal of earth from the top of it. It was located in the hole within the barn where it had been buried, specifically in the right-hand bay of the barn. The body had undergone varying degrees of decomposition in different areas. Based on my examination of the body, I would estimate that it had been in the ground for approximately nine or ten months or even longer, had I not been aware of it beforehand.

Various articles of clothing and personal items were found with the body, including stays, a flannel petticoat, a shift, a handkerchief tied around the neck, stockings, garters, high shoes, and remnants of a leghorn bonnet adorned with black trim. I have here a silk handkerchief that I removed from around the neck. The rest of the items are in such a deteriorated state that it's challenging to distinguish their material or form.

The body was positioned with the right hand resting on the right breast and appeared to be tightly packed together. It was that of a full-grown young woman. The condition of the face was severely degraded, but there were signs of blood, particularly on the right side of it.

Around her neck, I found a green striped handkerchief, which was tied in the usual manner but pulled extremely tight, forming a complete groove. It seemed intentionally tightened as if someone had deliberately pulled it. The tightness was such that I believe it could have caused strangulation, resulting in death. There was also a visible stab wound on the neck, about an inch and a half in length and extending deeply into the neck, though I couldn't determine which specific parts were affected due to the advanced state of decomposition.

Furthermore, there was a wound on the neck in the middle, resembling a wen. Additionally, there were signs of injuries to the right eye and the right side of the face. It appeared as though something had penetrated the eye socket, affecting the bone and the nose. This injury appeared to involve two separate actions: something entering from the left cheek and exiting through the right eye socket, along with a stabbing wound. It seemed as though an object, possibly a ball, had passed through the left cheek, removing the two last grinders.

The condition of the brain was so deteriorated that it was impossible to discern any specific details. I don't believe that a ball passing through on its own would have caused death, but in conjunction with the strangulation and the neck stab, it could have been lethal. The bone that separates the nostrils was completely broken and displaced, likely due to the passage of a projectile.

I performed an examination of the chest but did not find anything significant. There was an adhesion of the lung to the membrane lining the ribs on the right side, which, in life, would have caused inflammation and likely resulted in symptoms such as cough and side pain.

I also found two small pieces of bone in the throat, possibly from the interior of the nose, which might have fallen through during decomposition. The left hand was detached from the body and had the appearance of a skeletal hand, a result of decomposition.

In my opinion, the injuries alone, without the presence of the handkerchief, may not have been immediately fatal, although inflammation might have developed, leading to potential complications. Since then, I have examined the heart and ribs, some of which were brought to my house by Mr. Nairn, a surgeon. It became apparent that something had penetrated between the 5th and 6th ribs, causing a stab in the heart that aligned with the opening in the ribs. This injury alone could have been fatal. I also noticed a corresponding mark on the shift, where the opening matched in size with that of the ribs. As for the stays, they were too decomposed to discern any openings if they had ever existed.

I have examined the sword presented, which appears to fit the wound through the ribs and the opening in the shift. It penetrated about two or three inches, with one part of the wound wider and the other narrower, corresponding to the sword's dimensions. The ribs were reasonably preserved, and it appeared as though the wound in the heart had been inflicted by an instrument like this sword. The sword also fit into a wound in the spheroidal sinus, penetrating about an inch.

Regarding the head wound with a bullet, it was later discovered that no bullet had been found in the barn. However, the bullet we spoke of was located in the black reticule containing the pistols. The bullet matched the hole, suggesting that the bullet injury likely occurred before the stab wounds.

Blood was found on the shift, stays, the handkerchief around the neck, a lawn handkerchief, and the silk handkerchief, and it also seemed to be present on the bonnet. I do not recall finding any part of a shawl.

Lastly, I removed the garters, which were made of narrow white tape. While handling one of the shoes, the foot became detached. Both the lower and upper jaws had a missing tooth. I can distinguish between the cavity of a tooth extracted while the person was alive and that of a tooth lost due to decay. The jaw I have here currently has two missing teeth—one on the left, which I believe fell out after death, and another that had been missing for quite some time.

Autopsy #2: Performed by Two Surgeons: Mr. Chaplin, and Mr. Nairne

After Maria Marten's remains had rested peacefully in Polstead Churchyard for more than five weeks, certain events occurred that raised suspicions about a possible deficiency in the chain of evidence related to her cause of death. As a result of the likelihood of shedding new light on the matter, Mr. Wayman, the coroner, convened a meeting with several professionals at the Cock Inn in Polstead on June 3rd. During this gathering, they discussed whether it was appropriate to exhume Maria's body. The outcome of their deliberations led to the unanimous decision to once again disturb the quiet resting place of Maria.

This resolution was executed with utmost secrecy in the early hours of the following morning. The impetus for this significant investigation stemmed from a particular incident. A person named Glover was discussing the murder with Mr. Chaplin, during which Mr. Chaplin mentioned that he didn't believe Maria had been struck by the small shot that seemed to have been fired. He further noted that Mr. Lorton, the surgeon who conducted the initial examination, had opined that a pistol bullet had entered the deceased's neck near the jugular vein, taking an oblique path through to the eye on the opposite side of her head.

In response, Glover asserted that regardless of whether the unfortunate girl had been shot or not, it was abundantly clear that she had been stabbed in the side. As no evidence to support this claim had been presented to the coroner previously, Mr. Chaplin inquired about the basis for Glover's statement. Glover explained that he had closely examined the clothing in which the body was discovered, revealing a significant tear in both the stays and chemise of the deceased. This tear appeared to have been inflicted simultaneously with a wide, sharp instrument, which strongly suggested that she had been stabbed.

Mr. Chaplin personally inspected the stays and other clothing items and confirmed the accuracy of the description. Upon verifying this, he promptly relayed the information to Mr. Wayman, the coroner. The reason these clothing cuts had not been detected during the initial investigation was that the garments had been thoroughly soaked with the putrid fluids that had oozed from the body while it was inside the Red Barn. These fluids were sticky and obscured the cuts.

The professional individuals present during the exhumation included Mr. Henry Chaplin, a Surgeon from Lavenham, Suffolk; Mr. Nairne, a Surgeon from Bedham, Essex; and Mr. Bewick, who assisted Mr. Lorton of Boxford. Once the body was taken out of the grave, it was positioned beside the grave, and the gentlemen immediately began examining the left side. They decided to focus on this area due to the cuts they had noticed in the stays and shift that had been removed from the deceased when she was discovered on April 19th.

The outcome of their investigation left no room for doubt that the murderer had undoubtedly employed a sharp instrument among other means of causing harm. It's worth noting, however, that prior to the exhumation, there had been a difference of opinion regarding whether a re-examination of the badly decomposed body would yield any useful information. Nevertheless, the majority of those involved decided to proceed with the experiment.

Upon examining the ribs on the left side of the body, they discovered that a sharp instrument had passed between two of them, creating a hole approximately two and a quarter inches wide. It was evident that this wound had been inflicted at the same time as the cuts in the stays and shift, as these incisions perfectly matched. The medical professionals then removed the heart of the deceased, which, considering the considerable time that had passed since her death, was remarkably well-preserved.

Upon inspecting the part of the heart that was adjacent to the ribs, they found a puncture corresponding to the points where the instrument had separated the ribs. This puncture had evidently been made with the same deadly weapon used for the other wounds. The consensus was that an instrument like the small sword that had been sharpened and turned into a carving knife by Mr. Offord of Hadleigh could have caused the cuts seen in the clothing and the wounds inflicted on the deceased's body.

The medical professionals removed the two ribs through which the knife had passed, as well as the heart. The heart was preserved in spirits and entrusted to Mr. Nairne for presentation at the prisoner's trial. A gentleman who had seen the stab wound on the side, indicated by a mark between the ribs, described its shape and size as resembling that of a sharp, and the puncture in the heart, which, it should be noted, somewhat resembled a barleycorn but was slightly longer.

During the exhumation, the only individuals present, apart from the medical professionals, were Mr. Balham, the parish clerk, and some men who assisted in lifting the coffin from the grave. This task was not very challenging due to the dryness and quality of the soil. The exhumation occurred between three and four o'clock in the morning to prevent any unwelcome intrusions that might have disrupted this important investigation. The operations were carried out by torchlight.

It is impossible to fully describe the spectacle and the distressing characteristics of this deteriorated remnant of a human body. Therefore, we chose to draw a veil over the scene and return the mutilated and disjointed remains to the chamber of death.

Events Leading Up to the Arrest of William Corder

On the Sunday preceding May 18th, which happened to fall on a Friday, Maria Marten first visited her father's cottage and then proceeded to her mother's house. They decided that the following day they would go to Ipswich for their wedding, but this plan did not materialize. Subsequently, they arranged to go on the following Thursday, but this too did not come to pass.

On Friday, May 18th, around noon, Corder visited Maria Marten's father's house while she was upstairs with her mother. He asked her to get ready and accompany him. She expressed her inability to go at that moment, to which he responded, "You've been let down several times, and you must go now." During their conversation, it was decided that Maria should pack her clothes into a bag, and Corder would transport them to a place known as the Red Barn, situated on his mother's farm. To avoid drawing attention, Maria was to wear male attire at her father's house, change into female clothing at the barn, and then proceed to Ipswich for the wedding.

He intended to demonstrate that Maria had packed various female clothing items into a large bag, without specifying them individually. Additionally, Maria placed a small basket within this larger bag, and inside the small basket, she included a smaller black velvet bag, commonly referred to as a reticule.

He should have clarified that before they departed and while they were discussing Maria's attire, Corder mentioned to her that Balliaro, the constable, had shown him a letter authorizing her arrest for allegedly having a bastard child. Corder stated that the constable would be called as a witness and confirm that he never had such a letter as the prisoner claimed, nor did he make any such communication to Corder as alleged.

As it happened, on the day they left old Marten's cottage to head to the Red Barn, a younger brother of the deceased Maria Marten, who was working near the Red Barn, saw the prisoner pass by at a short distance carrying a pickaxe on his shoulder, heading towards his (Corder's) mother's house. He must now inform them that the next encounter between the prisoner and Maria Marten's mother-in-law occurred at Corder's mother's house. During this encounter, there was no significant interaction between them.

On the Sunday that followed, he visited her house and admitted that he hadn't actually married her daughter yet, even though he had taken her away for that purpose. He explained that they were waiting for the marriage license which needed to be sent to London. Additionally, he mentioned that her daughter was staying in Yarmouth under the protection of one of his female relatives.

Later in the same week, they had another meeting, during which she informed him that her son had seen him on the previous Friday near the Red Barn, carrying a pickaxe on his shoulder. In response, he said, "It couldn't have been me he saw; it must have been Acres, who was working that day near the barn." They planned to summon Acres as a witness, and he would confirm that he wasn't working there at that time or any time around then.

From that point onward until the discovery of the incident, Corder had frequent interactions with Maria Marten's parents.

Corder had been away from Polstead for an extended period, and on his return, he provided updates about Maria Marten, stating that she was residing with his friend Roland in Yarmouth. When questioned about her well-being, he assured them that she was in good health. In response to inquiries about why she hadn't written, he sometimes explained that she was too occupied, and on other occasions, he mentioned she had a sore on the back of her hand that had become infected, preventing her from using her fingers and, consequently, from writing.

Between May 18th and harvest time, Corder engaged in numerous conversations with various individuals concerning Maria Marten. Interestingly, he provided these people with different accounts of her compared to what he had told her father and mother. To one person, he claimed that she had departed via a steamboat to France, while to another, he stated that she was living nearby.

A particular conversation on this subject took place with a woman named Stow, who will be called upon as a witness. During this conversation, he informed her that Maria Marten was not residing far from their location. In the course of their discussion, she inquired if Maria Marten was likely to have more children. He responded with, "No, she won't. Maria Marten won't have any more children."

Mrs. Stow promptly asked him why not, pointing out that Maria Marten was still quite young. In reply, he insisted, "No, believe me, she won't have anymore; she's had her share." Mrs. Stow then inquired, "Is she far from here?" To which he replied, "No, she's not far from us; I can visit her whenever I want, and I'm aware that when I'm not with her, nobody else is."

There was a minor detail that might have been related to the events of May 18th, and he would now briefly explain it. During that time, the prisoner borrowed a spade from a woman named Stow. She couldn't recall the exact date when he borrowed it, but there were circumstances that suggested it was around the middle of May. It's worth noting that she had recently given birth to a child, and the spade was borrowed during the period between her recovery from childbirth and her churching. They would have the opportunity to hear her testimony and draw their own conclusions.

Moving forward in the narrative, the counsel proceeded to discuss the events that occurred in September of the same year. During this time, Corder was involved in directing the laborers to commence the harvest. In the weeks leading up to May 18th, the barn had mostly been empty, except for the old litter covering the floor. When the wheat was ready to be harvested, Corder instructed that the harvested grain should be stored in the upper bay of the barn. He personally oversaw the process when the first and second loads were brought in.

The keys to the barn were always kept at his mother's house. Additionally, the barn was not easily accessible because it was surrounded by various outbuildings and could only be reached through a gate that was seven feet high.

Once the harvested grain had been stored in the barn, Corder departed from Polstead. He was given a ride to Colchester by a man named Bright. During this journey, he provided Bright with a different account of Maria Marten compared to what he had told others. Specifically, he claimed that he hadn't seen her since the previous May.

Before leaving Polstead on that occasion, he had a conversation with Maria Marten's father. During this conversation, Corder mentioned that he looked forward to seeing his daughter soon. He also informed him that he had purchased a new set of clothes in preparation for their upcoming marriage.

Around October 19th or 20th, old Marten received a letter from the prisoner, which had the London postmark. In this letter, the prisoner claimed that he had married Maria. He also expressed surprise that the old man had not responded to the letter Maria had sent him after her marriage. In her letter, she supposedly mentioned that during their wedding, Mr. Roland played a fatherly role, and Miss Roland served as the bridesmaid. The prisoner requested an immediate reply and instructed the old man to send it to a specific address in the city using certain initials.

The father replied to the letter, stating that no such letter as described had ever been received. Corder then wrote back, explaining that he had inquired at the Post Office about the missing letter, and there were no records of it in the Post Office books in London. He believed the letter was lost because it had to cross the sea, as Maria was on the Isle of Wight when she wrote it.

In November of the previous year, the prisoner had an encounter with a gentleman named Matthews in London. During their correspondence, which he intended to present as evidence, Corder informed Matthews that he hadn't married Maria Marten yet due to some unresolved family matters. However, he mentioned that he was currently residing with her on the Isle of Wight.

As time passed, Maria Marten's parents did not receive any further communication from her, which made them increasingly concerned and suspicious about her well-being. These suspicions continued to grow, eventually taking a definite form. Their concerns were particularly focused on the Red Barn. Maria Marten's father developed a strong desire to investigate it, and in April of the current year, he went to the barn and conducted a search. At that time, the corn had already been threshed, but the old litter remained inside the barn.

They searched several locations within the barn, eventually focusing on the upper bay, where the ground seemed less stable than in other areas. Consequently, they decided to dig, and within about a foot and a half from the surface, they discovered the body of a female. The body was partially clad in female attire, including remnants of a jean pair of stays, a shift, and a flannel petticoat. Beneath the body, they found a handkerchief, and a green silk handkerchief was draped around the neck.

The body and clothing were closely examined by Maria Marten's father, mother, and sister. These witnesses would provide the jury with descriptions of the various marks on Maria's body. They would also discuss the natural marks found on the body in the barn. Maria Marten had a prominent growth or wen on her neck's midsection, and the same feature was observed on the female whose body was discovered in the barn. Additionally, Maria had lost two of her front teeth, a trait shared with the female whose body was found in the barn. The features of the body were not entirely decomposed, and the jury would hear the witnesses' accounts on that matter. Furthermore, the witnesses would detail the different components of Maria Marten's attire, focusing on her stays and neck handkerchief.

Maria Marten, when she was alive, experienced pain in her side and was suffering from asphyxia. The surgeons who examined the body found in the barn would testify that they observed significant signs of inflammation on one side of that body. I should inform the jury that the body discovered in the barn remained in the ground until the surgeon had a chance to inspect it. The examining surgeon would explain that they found a pistol ball lodged in the face, a wound in the neck inflicted by a sharp instrument, another wound on the face caused by a similar instrument, and a third wound of the same nature situated between the fifth and sixth ribs, which had penetrated the heart.

The first surgeon who examined the body removed the green silk handkerchief from the neck and confirmed that it must have been tightly bound around the neck, potentially causing death by strangulation. Consequently, suspicion immediately fell upon the prisoner in the dock. Information about the murder was promptly relayed to London. An astute police officer was tasked with apprehending the prisoner, and due to his efforts, the prisoner was arrested at a residence in Ealing.

The prisoner was apprehended at a residence in Ealing. Upon first encountering the prisoner, the officer informed him that he had come to arrest him on a very grave charge, nothing less than the murder of Maria Marten. The officer inquired if the prisoner knew such a woman, to which the prisoner replied that he did not. The officer then asked, "Have you never known Maria Marten?" The prisoner once again responded, "No, never."

The prisoner then attempted to suggest that there might be a mistake in his identity, saying, "You must be mistaken about the person you've come to arrest." The officer insisted, "No, I'm not mistaken about the person; your name is Corder, I believe." The prisoner confirmed that it was indeed his name. The officer repeated his question, "Did you never know Maria Marten?" and once more, the prisoner replied, "Never."

The officer warned the prisoner, saying, "I've asked you the question twice, and I will only ask you a third time: Did you never know Maria Marten?" For the third time, the prisoner responded, "Never." Subsequently, the officer arrested him.

During the arrest, the officer conducted a search of the house where the prisoner was residing. In one of the rooms, he discovered a small black velvet bag. The bag had a distinctive feature—it was lined with old silk and had a broad selvage around the rim. Mrs. Marten, as per his instructions, would later identify this bag as belonging to Maria Marten. Inside the bag, a pair of pistols was also found.

Case Summary:

Many months had passed since Maria Marten had left her home in a strange and suspicious manner. There had been no definite news about her, aside from some vague and unsatisfactory information provided by a man named Corder. This situation naturally caused great concern and alarm for Maria's father and his family. Adding to their worry, Corder had disappeared from Polstead for several months.

As days and months went by without any word from Maria, the anxiety grew. This was particularly troubling because Maria was known to be literate and had a strong bond with her family, especially her father and her young son. As Christmas approached, the Marten family became increasingly worried due to Corder's absence and the realization that he had been dishonest about Maria's whereabouts.

Corder consistently claimed that Maria was well and happy when asked, and he even once mentioned that she was staying with someone named Miss Rowland near Yarmouth. However, this turned out to be a blatant lie upon investigation. The distressed father, torn between skepticism and hope, wondered why Maria hadn't written to them. Corder offered various vague excuses, including the claim that her right hand was injured, preventing her from writing.

Corder always seemed to have an explanation whenever questioned closely. When asked about the urgency of Maria's trip to Yarmouth immediately after leaving home on May 18th, he explained that he had intended to marry her the next day but had discovered an issue with the marriage license, requiring him to go to London for a signature, which would delay the wedding by three weeks. After this time had passed, he continued to insist that he had married Maria.

Maria's mysterious disappearance had persisted for about ten months, with Corder also being absent for most of that time. Her family couldn't stop discussing her situation, constantly going over the details of her departure and the Red Barn incident. The more they discussed it, the more mysterious it seemed.

Finally, Ann Marten, Maria's stepmother approached her husband and said, "I have frequently dreamed about Maria, twice before Christmas and once after. I dreamed that Maria was murdered, and buried in the Red Barn." Mr. Marten asked, why did you not tell me this before?" Mrs. Marten replied I thought you would think that I am being superstitious. Some weeks passed without any more consideration about her dreams. Finally, she approached her husband again and suggested, "If I were in your place, I would go and inspect the Red Barn." She explained that she had dreamt about Maria several times, including two dreams before Christmas in which Maria was murdered and buried in the Red Barn. She hadn't shared this earlier because she feared her husband would think it superstitious.

Initially, Mr. Marten didn't take the suggestion seriously, but his wife persisted, and eventually, he went to the Red Barn with a man named Bowtell to investigate. They noticed that a portion of the earth in the barn's floor seemed less solid than the rest. Upon closer examination, they found loose soil that was relatively easy to remove. After digging about a foot and a half deep, they uncovered what appeared to be a human body wrapped in a sack. A green silk handkerchief was sticking out of the sack, though it had largely decayed due to the corpse's putrefaction. This green silk handkerchief belonged to Corder and was the one Maria had when she left her father's house.

Mr. Marten didn't open the grave further but returned home to inquire about the handkerchief Maria wore around her neck on the day she left. The response was "a green one." At that moment, the distraught father realized that Maria had been murdered, and his wife's ominous dreams had come true.

Upon this shocking revelation, the authorities were alerted, and a thorough investigation into Maria Marten's disappearance and murder was launched. Suspicion naturally fell on William Corder, the man who had been the last to see Maria alive and who had provided inconsistent and false information about her whereabouts.

Corder was swiftly apprehended and brought to trial for the murder of Maria Marten. The trial captured the public's attention and became a sensational case in the early 19th century in England.

During the trial, the gruesome details of Maria's murder were revealed. Corder had lured her to the Red Barn under the pretense of marriage. There, he shot her and buried her body in the barn. The green silk handkerchief served as a chilling piece of evidence, linking him directly to the crime scene.

The trial resulted in Corder's conviction, and he was sentenced to death. On August 11, 1828, he was executed by hanging.

Maria Tells Her Story

Although Corder was found guilty of murdering Maria Marten, he had an invisible accomplice that went unpunished. As I sat in my dimly lit family room with my Apple computer on my lap, I closed my eyes and invited the spirit of Maria Marten to share her story if she so desired. Soon after my invitation, a petite lady, with big brown eyes and dark curls peeking out from beneath her bonnet, appeared to me and introduced herself as Maria Marten. Almost immediately, she began to share the haunting tale of her tragic end.

In a soft tone of voice, she said:

"It was not solely William Corder who orchestrated my demise, but a malevolent force that clung to his very soul. After I had my William's baby a darkness seemed to gradually envelop him. I believe an evil spirit whispered wicked thoughts into his mind and clouded his love for me with malice. It was as if an unseen hand guided him, puppeteering his actions with a cruel and calculated intent. He seemed to be tormented, caught in a web of influence beyond his control. The evil spirit exploited his weaknesses, turning him into a vessel for its insidious desires.

He led me to the Red Barn under the influence of an evil spirit and as we stood in the shadows of the barn the presence of this ominous spirit was as palpable as the beat of my racing heart within my chest. William's eyes which were once filled with warmth and love, were now vacant, consumed by the darkness that held him captive. It was as if he were possessed, a mere instrument for the malevolent spirit's gruesome plan."

Maria proceeded to show me a vision of how the evil spirit murdered her using William as its channel to do so. As Maria's story unfolded, I could feel the evilness of the ancient supernatural forces that had destroyed the lives of Maria Marten and William Corder.

In the vision, I saw William and Maria standing in the middle of the barn. They appeared to be arguing. With a diabolical grin on William's face, he grabbed Maria and drew her to him in an embrace, not one of affection, but one designed to trap her. With his left arm around her waist, he pulled a pistol out of the right pocket of his coat with his right hand and placed it at the base of her jaw. He pulled the trigger and upon discharge of the bullet, Maria fell to the ground. At this point, she was not dead. The gurgling sound of her respirations seemed to throw William into a fit of rage. He took Maria's green bandana from her carpet bag and used it to strangle her thereby silencing her irritating respirations.

Using what looked like a pick-axe, he quickly dug a small and shallow grave on the far side of the barn near a wall. Once the grave was dug, he walked over to the body of Maria and stabbed her in the neck with the pick-axe. He used the axe to drag Maria's body to the grave. He pulled the axe out of her neck and stabbed her on the left side of the chest so that he could roll her torso into the grave.

After showing me this vision, Maria said, "Do not condemn him, for he, too, was a victim of evil forces. I am free from the oppression of the evil spirit that murdered me. I hope that William's soul will soon be released too. Please let the world know that William is an innocent victim as I was. He did not murder me. It was the evil spirit that took control of his body that killed me." As the connection with Maria's spirit waned, I was left with a profound sense of responsibility to reveal the truth about the evil spirit's influence and bring closure to the tormented souls of Maria Marten and William Corder.

~ 3 ~

CASE FILE #2: HELEN JEWETT-A HIGH CLASS NYC PROSTITUTE

Helen Jewett
Public Domain

Case Summary

Name of Deceased: Helen Jewett

Before taking the name Helen Jewett, she also went by Dorcas Doyen, Dorcas Dorrance, Maria G. Benson, Ellen Spaulding, Helen Mar, and Maria Stanley, however, Dorcas Doyen was probably her real name.

Date of Birth: circa January 1812

Location of Birth: Two locations are cited in the popular literature: Hallowell, Maine, and Augusta Maine

Date of Death: April 10, 1836

Location of Death: Rosina Townsend's boarding house in New York City, New York.

Deceased Found by: Rosina Townsend

Relationship to the Deceased: Landlady

Complainant: Rosina Townsend

Witnesses: Rosina Townsend found the body, but did not see the assailant.

Estimated Time of Death: Between midnight and 3 a.m.

Position of Body: The victim was found on her back in bed with her head on the left side

Wounds: A deep wedge-shaped laceration to the right side of her head, along with a couple of superficial cuts. She was charred on the entire left-hand side of her body and the anterior aspect of her right leg.

Autopsy Findings: Results of the autopsy indicated that the victim died from a blow to the head with a heavy object by the hand of another. The force of the fatal blow caused immediate death.

Disposition: Cold Case—Richard P. Robinson was found not guilty a sympathetic jury.

Background Informant Source: (The) Authentic Biography of the Late Helen Jewett, a Girl of the Town Who was Murdered on the 10th of April, 1836: Together With a Full and Accurate Statement of the Circumstances Connected With That Event by a Gentleman Fully Acquainted With Her History. (1836). New York.

Background on the Murder of Helen Jewett

The real name of the beautiful and unfortunate Helen Jewett was Dorcas Doyen. Her parents were Welsh but had emigrated to this country at an early period of marriage, and at the time of the birth of their only daughter, they resided in the outskirts of Augusta, in the state of Maine. Their circumstances were humble, the father being a mechanic, dependent on his daily labor for this subsistence, and the mother subject to tasks of knitting and shoe-binding to supply the deficits sometimes occasioned by her husband's drunken sprees.

Dorcas, their child, was born in June. Her father, at the time of her birth, was connected with a man by the name of Caleb Talbot, in the Lumber business, and was supposed to be in good circumstances; but the elopement of his partner, with the proceeds of a large sale of lumber, and with some four or five thousand dollars belonging to the firm, which had been deposited in the State Bank at Boston, rendered him bankrupt.

He died about a year after the birth of Dorcas, leaving his wife and child in extremely indigent circumstances. For several years after this event, Mrs. Doyen, who was a woman of extraordinary personal beauty, supported herself and her child by teaching a country school. Notwithstanding her poverty, she bestowed the greatest attention upon the education of Dorcas, who attracted the attention of all her acquaintances by her beauty, vivacity, good temper, and quickness of apprehension. Indeed, so rapid was the development of her mental qualities, that at the age of five years, she had made mere progress in the usual studies, than the generality of children at twice her age.

About this time, she attracted the attention of some of the members of Judge Western's family, who resided in Augusta, about two miles from Hallowell. They, like all others who knew her, were particularly pleased with her beauty, docility, and acuteness of intellect.

Through their interest, she enjoyed the advantages of attending a select school in Augusta, at which she made the most astonishing progress in her studies. When she was about six years of age, her mother died. She was then taken into Judge Western's family, and treated in every respect as a member of it. She was sent to the same schools and pursued the same studies and employment as his own children. She remained under his roof until the summer of 1826, when she, with a daughter of Judge Western, of the same age, was sent to Portland, to attend a female seminary, which was under the charge of a Mrs. Watson, who by her talent and admirable management, had acquired for her school considerable celebrity.

This departure from the immediate surveillance of her kind friends may be traced to her first misfortune, which resulted in her expulsion from society, a life of infamy and guilt, and her untimely and horrible end. No person could have been better qualified to take charge of females of her age, and to direct their minds in the paths of honor and usefulness, than Mrs. Watson. But, unfortunately, the building occupied by Mrs. W. as a seminary, was not sufficiently large to accommodate the whole of her numerous school as boarders. Many of her pupils from a distance, as well as those residing in the town, were compelled to board outside of the walls of the seminary, which they attended only as day scholars. Of course, she could not keep as strict a watch on their conduct as if they had resided in her family—a circumstance, which, in Maria's case, is much to be regretted.

At the house in which Maria boarded, (kept by a Mrs. Wilson) there were several other boarders, and among the rest, a man by the name of Lemuel Lawton, who was at that time studying law. He was tall, good-looking, and of an exceedingly insinuating address but wholly destitute of principle or moral worth. At that period, however, he bore a very good character, but subsequent events, particularly some frauds in the mercantile business to which he afterward turned his attention, together with one or two other seduction cases, have proven his utter depravity. From his first acquaintance with Maria, he bestowed upon her the most assiduous attention.

She was then particularly interesting, both to young and old. It was her fifteenth year, although in appearance she was somewhat older. With a form of the most perfect symmetry and beauty, her eyes brilliant and full of expression and intelligence, her cheeks glowing with the richest hues of youth and health—her manners and conversation frank, fascinating, and graceful, she excited the admiration of all who knew her.

Lawton's fancy was touched, as for heart, he had none, and he resolved to sacrifice her in all her youthful purity, upon the altar of licentiousness. Though at that time, but nineteen years of age, he was a veteran in vice; he boasted among his companions, of the laurels he had won in the field of Venus. With Maria, however, he was aware that the ordinary measures of the seducer would not succeed; and he acted upon the principle, *first debauch the mind and the person follows as a matter of course.* He employed himself in instilling into her mind the poison of his own vicious principles, and in eradicating what he endeavored to convince her were the prejudices of education. Upon all occasions, he was her constant attendant. He rode with her, walked with her, and attended her at patties, the church, and the sports of the neighborhood; in addition, he had daily opportunities to see her at home, in private. The writer was on one occasion, at a party where Maria and Lawton were both present and particularly noticed the attention which the latter bestowed upon her—she was then the most beautiful and fascinating girl he had ever seen. Lawton directed her taste for reading into new channels; and, among other books of immoral tendency, he introduced to her notice the glowing and luscious pages of the noble bard, who, as poor Maria has been heard to say,

Has done more injury to female minds than all other authors of the safe character combined. Don Juan, at length, under Lawton's direction, became her study. Its vivid images of the grossest licentiousness, half veiled in the charm of the poetry, worked upon her active imagination, excited her naturally ardent temperament, unsettled the principles of virtue, and disposed her, in an evil hour, to fall prey to her seducer's arts. Let not the rigid moralist condemn her until they have considered the peculiar circumstances of the case, and the improbability that almost any female could have resisted the temptations and deceitful illusions by which she was surrounded.

She had resided in Portland for more than a year before Lawton succeeded in his purpose. It cost him all this time of the most strenuous exertions to attain that which, owing to the defective system of female education, is too often granted to the slightest solicitation; and even then, it is supposed, he accomplished his object by the employment of a medical preparation. These facts speak strongly, considering her extreme youth, for her natural strength of mind.

The intercourse between Maria and Lawton had continued but a short time, before Maria became aware of its consequences—she was enciente (pregnant)! In a few months more, it was evident to all observers; and Mrs. Watson, after ascertaining the facts, communicated her knowledge to Judge Western, who, upon the receipt of the: intelligence, immediately hastened to Portland. In the meantime, the unfortunate Maria, overwhelmed with grief and shame, afraid to meet the guardian, whose confidence and kindness she had abused, and whose favor she had forfeited, threw herself into the arms of her seducer, in reckless defiance of public infamy, and clandestinely left Portland with him for Boston. After having arrived and found her gone, Judge Western ascertained the direction she had taken, commissioned a friend who was going on to Boston to find her out, and offered her a maintenance in some country place where, she was not known, provided she would return. This gentleman, several weeks after her elopement, discovered her in a house of ill fame, where she had been placed by Lawton. She had been delivered of a child, which survived only a few hours after birth. Maria was still confined to her bed from the effects of her accouchement when this gentleman conveyed Judge Western's proposition to her, which she vehemently refused. She stated that she did not consider, herself worthy of the favor of any of her friends, and all she wished was for them to forget her. She wrote a few lines to Judge Western to, the same effect—a copy of which the writer of this has seen,—and recollects the following expression: "I was dead to virtue—I am now dead to society, and it is my most earnest wish that I may be soon dead to nature."

Shortly after her recovery, Lawton left her and went to Alabama.

His lust had been satiated by her ruin, and her support was a tax and trouble which his selfishness would not allow him to endure. He left her utterly destitute. Of course, she was compelled to take up the trade of the house or be turned into the streets. She was induced to form a connection with General Calhoun, who kept her in a very handsome style in Boston for some time. He came to reside in this city in 1829, and brought her with him, when she, assumed the name of Helen Jewett. She lived with him here but a short time. He was exceedingly disagreeable in his manners, and she soon found an opportunity to form an advantageous connection.

She made the acquaintance of J. C., a wholesale merchant, who was so pleased with her beauty and conversational powers, that he made her the most liberal offers, which were accepted.

She was likewise kept for some time by Mr. C, a wealthy Southern gentleman. It would be useless and impossible to particularize her numerous paramours with whom: she lived as a regular kept mistress. In addition to this, she did a very lucrative miscellaneous business, not confined to this city, but occasionally taking short trips to Philadelphia and Boston. The most prominent residences at which she lived were Mrs. Post's, Ann Walden's—for whom she was housekeeper for some time—Rosina Townsend's, and a house on Franklin Street.

It cannot be said that she was perfectly faithful to her different keepers. She most generally had someone upon whom she bestowed her favor par amours, as she was a girl of ardent temperament, and strong passions, she took strong likes and dislikes to individuals of the male sex, but when she liked a person, she would spare no pains to secure for a while the object of her desire. The following is one of her letters written while she was kept by Mr. C. to a physician of this city, who was called to attend one of the girls of the house, and being struck with her evident intellect and education, had paid her a good deal of attention:

> New York, Howard Street
>
> My Dear Sir
>
> Allow me to say, dear, for I assure you are so to me. I think of nothing but you. You alone of all the creatures of your sex by whom I am surrounded, have evinced the least spark of real sympathy with my feelings, the least pity for my faults and misfortunes. You, I think are willing to believe that a woman may cast away the *immediate jewel of her soul* without becoming wholly depraved, or entirely losing the feelings and characteristics of her sex. Think, then, how anxious I must be for your society, and if you have the least spark of compassion for me come and see me as often as you can. You do not know what pleasure your acquaintance is to me; I shall always look upon it as the brightest spot in the later years of my existence—a single oasis in the vast desert of wretchedness, shame, guilt, blighted prospects, and perverted powers which I am compelled to call my life. Come and see me as soon as you can; I shall expect you every evening.
>
> Yours, truly, and forever,
>
> HELEN

The next letter was written sometime after the above: |t is to the same person, but in a different style.

> Dear T—,

What is the matter with you? Are you getting tired of me? What can be the reason that you have not been to see me for six whole days—almost a week—perhaps you don't know that six days are almost a week, I assure you they are, and a long one too in love's almanac, I am almost disposed to punish you for your negligence. I have half a mind to bore you with a whole ocean of sentiment about my own love and misery, and your selfishness and coldness—but I forbear. I'll spare you till next time. Come up and see me this evening. Don Alonzo has gone to Philadelphia. He wanted to take me with him. I was very much tempted to go but I thought of you and refused. Evince your gratitude, and let me behold the light of your countenance once more.

Adieu juaque les momenta delicieux,
A soubriquet for her keeper,
Helen

During all this time, it must not be supposed that Helen was solely engaged in scenes of debauchery. She found time to improve her mind in an intellectual way very much. She read a great deal, especially the light literature of the day: She was a subscriber to most of our literary periodicals. The works of Lord Byron were her study; she could repeat more than half of his writings by heart.

Her memory not only retained the words, but her whole mind seemed to be imbued with the spirit of his poetry. She sometimes composed poetry herself. Some of her pieces were remarkable for their easy and correct versification. The following lines, although not her best, are a very creditable specimen of her powers. They were written in answer to the question of why she secluded herself so much from society. They are only a fragment.

I leave a noisy joyous crowd

Who will not dim one smile

Nor bate a note of laughter loud,

Though I am gone the while.

Yet, am I lonely? No! To me,

My own sad thoughts are company.

Tis lonelier far, than so to sit,

Away from human sin;

To join a crowd, ye be of it,

A path, but not akin

Oh! Is it not sweater thus to be

Where my sad thoughts make company.

For a long time after Helen arrived in this city, she resisted the demoralizing influence of the profession to which she had devoted herself, with wonderful power. She carefully eschewed the use of spirituous liquors, profane swearing, and obscene language, although it must be confessed, that in the last year or two of her life, her natural delicacy and cultivated taste had, in a great degree, succumbed to the influence of the circumstances by which she was surrounded. She had lost much of her beauty in the last years of her life; although her form still retained its full rounded and voluptuous proportions. She was endowed with extraordinary muscular strength and a most fearless and independent spirit. Upon one occasion, at a house in this city where she was boarding, she quarreled with a foolish fellow who frequented the house. He got exceedingly angry and drawing a pistol, presented it to her breast.

Without being in the least agitated, she instantly struck the pistol from his hand, and with her bright eyes flashing fire, in tones calm and clear, indicative of the strongest contempt, she said to him, "You poor contemptible libel upon manhood! You have done what would disgrace the meanest, coward that walks the street. You must see, therefore, the necessity of making an immediate apology for such brutal conduct." Her opponent declared he would do no such thing."Then," said Helen, "You must see the necessity I am under of pulling your nose." Suiting the action to the word, she took the gentleman's proboscis in her fingers and tweaked it in no gentle style.

She was particularly remarkable for her powers of bitter, biting sarcasm. The way she served up, those who roused her ire was a caution to all her acquaintances, which they generally took care to attend. She appeared, upon one occasion, before the Police, to make a charge against a man by the name of Burk, an officer in the British army, who, out of revenge, had cut and destroyed her dresses. She walked up to him at the examination in great style. "You," she said, "pretend to be an officer in the British army! What a calumny upon His Majesty's service! You, an officer! It is impossible. The men holding his Majesty's commissions have generally some pretensions to the character of gentlemen."

One evening, when she: was housekeeper for, Ann Weldon, 'the public parlor being full of company, a poor devil attempted to be, particularly smart, by uttering the usual brothel witticisms, in the course of which, he said something which offended Helen, "What did you say?" she asked. "I can't find ears and talk too" he replied. "*Well," exclaimed Helen, "I never particularly examined your ears, but to judge from your conversation, I should think they ought to be large enough and long enough to supply the whole company. Your conversation is as silly as it is disgusting. There is the door, Sir, and I beg you to do me the favor of never calling here again, as you will save me the trouble of ordering the servant to kick you into the street."

Upon another occasion, young H. B—a dandified jackass, well-known about town, was attempting to do the amiable to Helen in the most extravagant style. She made some retort to one of his observations, which cut him very severely. "Now really, Miss Helen," said he, it is too bad for you to be so hard upon me—it is a shame, upon honor." 'You are right," returned Helen; it is wrong in me to be hard upon so soft a subject—we never use diamonds to carve geese."

She was once up before one of our Courts as a witness in a case in which the woman with whom she boarded was a party. The council, Mr. F. J., who cross-examined her, asked her several impertinent and irrelevant questions, and among the rest, whether there were not many gentlemen in the habit of visiting the house:

"Yes"

"Well, what did they visit the house for?"

"To see the girls."

"But what did they want of the girls?"

"I believe there is no one better qualified than yourself to answer that question, as I have observed you frequently among our visitors: will you be so kind as to save me the trouble of answering the question, and communicate to the Court your own experience upon the subject." The learned counsel concluded he had caught a Tartar and backed out of the scrape, though with rather a bad grace.

On the whole, Helen Jewett was a most extraordinary individual. Under other and better circumstances, she would have proven to be an honor and an ornament to her sex. As it was, she can only be considered a brilliant and fascinating prostitute. How deeply is it to be regretted that a girl of her extraordinary mental powers should not have had the watchful guardianship of a mother, at a time when the passions are bursting forth in their full strength—the judgment yet in abeyance, and the moral principle weak.

Account of the Murder

Never before has a similar event caused such a sensation and excitement in the public mind as the murder of Helen Jewett. The unusual circumstances of the case—the gruesome manner of the crime, the character, talents, and fame of the victim, and the youth and status of the alleged murderer—have all contributed to this reaction. The public's curiosity has been strongly aroused, eager to know every detail of the bloody incident.

A few days before her murder, Helen moved from a house on Franklin Street, where she had been living, to stay with Rosina Townsend, with whom she had previously lived. The murder occurred between midnight and 3 AM on April 10th. A coroner's inquest was summoned as soon as possible. According to the testimony of Rosina and other witnesses before the coroner's jury, around 9 PM on Saturday evening, a young man named Richard P. Robinson, a clerk for Mr. Joseph Hoxie, arrived at the house. He was met by Rosina and asked for Helen Jewett, one of the girls of the house, whom he had been visiting regularly since 1834. Rosina called Helen from the parlor, and she and Robinson went upstairs to her room.

Nothing more was heard from them until 11 PM, when Helen came partway downstairs and asked Rosina, the landlady, to bring a bottle of champagne to her room. Rosina did so, finding Robinson in bed undressed, while Helen, also undressed, had not yet gone to bed. Neither of them was seen again by any of the house's inhabitants when Rosina closed the house for the night around midnight.

About three o'clock in the morning, Rosina was aroused by knocking at her front door, and on looking out of her window, discovered the person at the door to be a young man who was in the habit of visiting one of the girls, and she went to the door and let him in. In doing this, she was surprised to find in her front parlor a lamp burning, which she knew from the fact that she had but two like it in the house, to belong to Helen, or the girl in the room adjoining. She took it upstairs and by gently shaking the door adjoining Helen's found it locked. Then, she took the ring of keys out of her pocket and upon unlocking the door, was almost suffocated by the great body of smoke which instantly rushed out. The room was on fire. She instantly alarmed everyone with a cry that the house was on fire; and Helen was smothering or dead. Running down to the front door, she cried for watchmen, two or three of whom were soon on the spot.

She ran back upstairs and opened the windows so that the smoke could escape, the bed and bedding were almost completely consumed, and Helen was lying on it dead. Her left side, head to foot, was charred black. At first, it was not obvious that anything more than the fire and smoke caused her death; but one of the watchmen happened to look more closely and discovered that there was, on the right side of her head a little above the temple, a large and deep cut, about three inches in length. On further inspection, the cut appeared to have been made with some sharp instrument in the shape of an axe or hatchet, which penetrated her skull and entered the brain instantly killing her. She probably wasn't even aware that she had been struck. Two other superficial cuts were found near the deep wound, but it appeared that she only received one fatal blow. A bottle of champagne which was brought up earlier that evening by Rosina, was standing on the mantelpiece, nearly empty. Except for the bed and curtains, the other furniture in the room remained unburned. Robinson, who had been in the room with Helen earlier that night, was nowhere to be found.

Upon inspecting the backyard, a hatchet was found with a string attached to it The hatchet had a significant amount of fresh blood on both thc blade and handle, One of the watchmen who climbed to the top of the fence discovered a black cloth cloak lying in the second yard over. This cloak was similar to the one Robinson wore to the house that evening. Upon examining the cloak, a string identical in size and appearance to the one attached to the hatchet was found tied to one of the cloak's tassels.

The reasonable inference is that Robinson brought the hatchet to the house with the intention of killing Helen. To conceal the hatchet, he suspended it inside the cloak by the tassel. In his panic to escape, Robinson likely dropped both the hatchet and the cloak in different places, possibly without realizing he had lost them.

Upon making these discoveries, the Coroner was called to the scene of the tragedy and arrived between five and six o'clock. After hearing what had happened, he sent a messenger to fetch Officer Brink, who lived a few blocks away. When Mr. Brink arrived, he was sent to pursue Robinson. Brink went to Robinson's boarding house on Day Street and was shown to Robinson's room, where he found Robinson in bed with his roommate, apparently fast asleep. Brink woke Robinson and informed him that he needed to get up and come with him. As Robinson dressed, Brink noticed that there was a significant amount of whitewash on one of the legs and the seat of Robinson's pants. It was also discovered that one of the fences Robinson must have climbed over before dropping his cloak was whitewashed on one side.

When Robinson was brought to the scene of the tragic event, he looked at the lifeless, burned, and disfigured body of his paramour with great composure and claimed he knew nothing about her murder or the circumstances surrounding it. Nevertheless, the Coroner committed him to Bridewell to await further investigation of this terrible affair.

Robinson's roommate, an intelligent young man, testified before the Coroner. He said he went to bed around nine o'clock on Saturday evening and fell asleep, not hearing Robinson come in or knowing when he went to bed. During the night, he awoke and found Robinson in bed, though not asleep. When he asked Robinson how long he had been in bed, Robinson replied that he came to bed around half past eleven. The cloak found in the neighboring yard was not proven to belong to Robinson, who typically wore a camblet cloak. However, his roommate admitted that he recognized the cloak and had seen Robinson wear it before.

The coroner's charge was that the deceased died from a blow to the head with a hatchet, inflicted by Richard P. Robinson. Although circumstantial evidence strongly implicates Robinson as the murderer, many people find it hard to believe he committed the crime. If Robinson is indeed the murderer, one would naturally consider the motives behind such a horrific act. However, none of the usual motives seem to be present in this case. The deceased had mentioned to the house's mistress on Tuesday night that Frank Rivers was going to get married, had returned her letters, and wanted his letters back. It was also said that he sometimes expressed dissatisfaction when he visited and found her with other men. On the other hand, the deceased was reportedly very attached to him and was showing his portrait to her friends the day before she was murdered. This portrait, along with the letters he had written to her and the ones she had written to him, was found among the deceased's belongings at Robinson's lodgings.

From these letters, it was discovered that Frank Rivers was actually Robinson. The letters were addressed to Robinson on the outside, but inside, they were written to "Dear Frank." The lack of clear motives strongly suggests Robinson's innocence. In fact, the only way to understand how a young man like him could commit such a crime is to assume there is some unknown cause or that he has a unique mental condition beyond the comprehension of an average person.

The Letters

Rhode Island
October 3rd 1836.

In presenting this confidential letter from my schoolmate, the unfortunate and persecuted Richard P. Robinson, to the public, I might be criticized by the biased as a meddlesome person asserting my right as an American citizen to think and act according to my judgment, defying a group of Editors who, like a pack of bloodhounds, have united to hunt down a nineteen-year-old boy to the death. This persecution is merely because a brothel keeper accused him of a crime they could not prove, and of which twelve respectable citizens have declared him innocent. The gentlemen who made this judgment have since been criticized for not wrongfully depriving an honorable family of one of its members. Let the Sun beware, as a reckoning is impending that could cause a downfall. I will say nothing more for now; the creator of the moon story is capable of any deception to serve his interests. My sole aim in publishing this letter from my youthful friend, who shared my childhood joys, is to encourage charitable thoughts towards him and to urge fair-minded individuals to judge his faults for themselves. I sincerely hope my humble effort is successful and that time will bring the truth to light.

Your Humble Servant,
Thomas Armstrong.

Dear Tom,

Knowing that you, among many others, do not consider me guilty is a relief beyond what you can imagine amidst all my suffering. By confessing all my wrongdoings to you now, I hope to reinforce your belief in my innocence regarding the terrible crime I am accused of. I have done bad things, but thank God, my hands are free of blood, and my conscience is clear of seduction! Emma T. was the seducer, not the seduced; but she is married, and her reputation must remain untarnished. Her name will never pass my lips nor be written by my pen. Now, I will give you a clear and honest account of all my wrongdoings during my time in New York, which have ended so disastrously. I have found a safe refuge, far from the persecution of the editorial corps that attacked me, and here I will stay until the true perpetrators of Ellen's death are brought to light.

Your sincere friend,
Richard P. Robinson

Richard Robinson's Address to the Public

Since the earliest days of civilization, where moral laws are practiced, it has been customary that when an accused person, regardless of the crime, has been tried and found not guilty, their punishment should end. This principle aligns with our glorious constitution and the right to a fair trial by jury, which is man's greatest privilege. After standing the test of public investigation, and with no strong proof of guilt, the accused should be shielded from further punishment or slander, regardless of the charges brought against their life or reputation by chance, envy, or necessity.

This custom was followed in all nations until my unfortunate case occurred this year. If I could have easily accounted for my whereabouts on the fatal Saturday night when Ellen was sacrificed to vile jealousy, it would be a simple matter. However, being aware of my innocence in this cruel transaction and horrified by the sight of a beautiful girl I loved, now a mangled corpse, my spirit recoiled from the false accusation. Shocked and irritated, I treated the baseless charge and its inventors with the contempt they deserved. The only rational response I gave was to Mrs. Gallagher, asking what motive I could possibly have to ruin my brilliant prospects and make my family miserable for life. This seemed to momentarily silence Mrs. Townsend, and I said no more, trusting in the fair laws of my country and the sound judgment of my fellow citizens on the jury.

This silence offended many, but to my friends, I provided a clear and detailed account of how and where I spent the evening until eleven o'clock when Ellen let me in after her first visitor left. Mrs. Townsend swore it was me, and it was true that I was in the house when the champagne was brought up.

But I had only been there for fifteen minutes. Helen informed me in a note that she was expecting a wealthy new admirer that evening, who would use my fictitious name. She said he wouldn't stay long, and I could enter as he was leaving. To facilitate this, she opened the front door for him herself and let me in unnoticed by the rest of the household. I intended to end my association with Helen and her disreputable circle, as I had developed a sincere and holy love for an amiable girl, which had completely changed my feelings. I looked back in horror at the path of vice, infamy, and degradation I had followed since arriving in New York.

To explain the depravity of my early life might partially atone for the harm I've done to my family and satisfy the curiosity of those who so eagerly sought my downfall. I was at an age when passions began to dominate the human experience. Imagine the temptations I faced at barely fifteen, being ardent, tender, rather handsome, well-dressed, and with money at my disposal. I quickly became an object of attraction for the young women who roamed the streets of New York, seeking admiration and believing that everyone who looked at them was enamored with their charms and ready to worship them.

Enchanted by the beauty of Emma T—, a girl who was poor, vain, and selfish, and who believed I was a wealthy gentleman's son with high prospects, she sought to entangle me in a secret marriage. Our initial meeting happened at night in the street, but I had encountered her several times during the day in various places, whether by chance or by her design, exchanging smiles of recognition. Our interactions were familiar, like those of old acquaintances. She accompanied me to a confectioner's shop where I spent money freely, finding pleasure in her company.

After that, we met every evening. I took her to public gardens and showered her with gifts of clothing, trinkets, and money. At her suggestion, I attended a dancing school where she had become a student at my expense. In the lively atmosphere of the ballroom, I noticed her being admired by all the ladies and observed her flirtatious behavior with everyone. It didn't take long for me to realize that Emma lacked gratitude, as well as feelings of prudence.

As time passed and I matured, I realized that Emma was looking for a husband and would marry the first man who offered. Despite her numerous obligations to me, this behavior hastened her downfall. I had already committed theft from my employer for her sake, one crime leading to another, and this ultimately led to me being labeled her seducer, although her willingness was as evident as mine.

Over time, the impact of our relationship became evident, and she moved into a boarding house with Ellen Jewett. This was a private boarding house for young ladies with strong financial support from their families. I paid ten dollars a week for her board, not including her extravagant other expenses. I often shrank back and trembled when she demanded the most expensive clothing, jewelry, diamonds, pearls, and trinkets. I never refused her requests because she threatened to expose me to my employers and incite her family to prosecute me for seducing her. Reading the tragedy of George Barnwell would show my situation clearly, and her behavior was akin to the character of Millwood before she turned sixteen. Initially, I would sneak into her room and wait for her, but she soon grew tired of solitude and began going to the theatre, which I had to accompany her to.

Our first visits to the theatre were in the second-tier boxes, but she disliked the decorum required in proper society. One evening, when I wasn't with her, she debuted in the third tier with Helen. She fell ill and had to be taken home in a carriage, and her life was in jeopardy for weeks. During her illness, Ellen cared for her like a kind-hearted sister, reassuring me of her recovery. There were rumors of a stillborn child, but I'm uncertain of its fate. During Emma's sickness, I became acquainted with other women in similar situations, and I generously gave them gifts of silks, velvets, and clothes. I gained favor with the whole family, spending nights with various respectable men who, despite their public personas of morality, indulged in vice and violated principles of chastity and virtue.

If the secret dealings of New York City were exposed, the depth of depravity would shock everyone! It would rival the wickedness of Sodom and Gomorrah. The servants mimic their employers' vices, laughing at morals, sobriety, honesty, and hard work. Property owners exploit tenants to fund their extravagance, and in turn, servants retaliate when they can. I felt no guiltier than others in this environment. For instance, look at the freedom young Onderdonk enjoyed under his father's watchful eye, while I, an unprotected boy without connections to introduce me to respectable circles, was left to my own devices in a boarding house where I had freedom after work hours. Mr. Hoxie, my employer, never questioned my nights; as long as I performed well at the store, he cared little about my conduct elsewhere. My sad story should serve as a warning to parents in the countryside about sending their sons into the temptations of vice without guidance or supervision. If merchants' apprentices were placed under proper supervision, fewer might fall into disgrace and end up in prison.

When a youth used to the comforts and discipline of home finds himself suddenly in the allurements of New York, with loose cash and little oversight, it's no surprise if he tries to increase his income discreetly. This was my situation when I met Helen Jewett. Unlike many women of her profession in New York, Helen lacked the usual brashness and vulgarity. Raised in a refined family in Maine, she associated with well-bred girls and had a sophisticated mind and taste. Although she could behave like a lady, there were moments when her anger revealed a coarser side. Helen was also skilled in needlework, industrious, kind-hearted, and well-read. These qualities, along with her refinement and artistic interests, set her apart from others in her circle. Only a brute and a villain would insult her, and only a truly evil person would take her life.

It was during Emma's illness that my relationship with Helen began, with no thought of any other connection between us. She was a comforting angel to me during that time. When Emma recovered, Helen took her to the countryside, posing as her sister and leaving her in the care of a respectable family. Emma's illness, her extravagant behavior, and especially her ignorance, had caused me to lose all affection for her. I fell deeper into a lifestyle of debauchery, going from one girl to another until I had a collection like the Grand Turk's harem, choosing only the ones I wanted to be with.

Helen's return brought me back to reality. She warned me about the physical toll my actions were taking on my health and the risk of being exposed if I continued to lavish expensive gifts on those who might betray me. This alarmed me and made me more cautious about how I distributed the ill-gotten gains among the girls. I became fully attached to Helen, despite her being older than me, loving her as much as a young man in my position could love someone of her background.

Helen became familiar with all my personal affairs, my family, and my future prospects. She was not a greedy or dishonest person, but she had received substantial money from wealthy visitors and managed it wisely, saving a small fortune through investments and gambling. As her favored lover, I was privy to her financial dealings, including significant sums of money she kept and invested through a broker in New York.

As for Emma, her fate is a story I cannot tell without causing harm to a family. Helen used all her cunning and influence to keep us apart, and she succeeded. Whether she ever hoped I would marry her, I cannot say, but she used every trick to win my affection, albeit unsuccessfully, as I was mindful of my family's respect and did not want to be entangled beyond what I could easily break free from. Despite receiving favors from Helen, I always repaid her.

My previous involvement with Emma had hardened me against Helen's charms. I knew she had power over me due to our shared secret ways of acquiring money, which benefited me without Mr. Hoxie losing anything. I feared offending her greatly, aware of her strong mind and noble spirit, even though she detested the lifestyle she had been led into by a villainous man. Money and jealousy were potent motives for crime, and it wouldn't surprise me if that man was implicated in her eventual demise. Helen and I often argued, resorting to letters when not on good terms. Initially, she could intimidate me into compliance by threatening exposure, but I eventually learned her tactics and stood up to her, leading to two years of wrongdoing, disgrace, and misery.

My association with Gray stemmed from my financial dealings with Helen. He became my agent, and we rented a room to conduct our business. Oh, the shady affairs that occur when a single gentleman rents private rooms, especially when there's no apparent business involved! Eventually, it seemed like my guardian angel had not entirely abandoned me. Love, a pure and holy love, filled my heart for a young lady, my equal in family and fortune but far superior in virtue. I looked up to her as the one who could lead me to a life of peace and domestic happiness. Though still young, barely past boyhood, I was already steeped in vice. Yet, I had a potentially long life ahead, albeit one I felt was too brief for redemption. I wasn't sure if my first employer suspected me, but I was certain Mr. Hoxie remained unaware of any losses I had caused.

My first step toward reform was cutting ties with Gray, which was easily justified by his marriage. This move alarmed Helen, who grew suspicious of my distancing from her control. I feigned concern about being suspected at work for visiting her house, leading her to change residences. When I objected to her new place as too exposed, she accused me of abandonment. I didn't deny it and demanded back a miniature painted for Emma. She refused, and our exchange of letters included threats from both sides, which my enemies later used against me.

Eventually, the storm of emotions settled, and we met by her invitation, reconciling and exchanging forgiveness. Helen wept on my shoulder, acknowledging the role of tears in preserving her sanity. She warned me to step back from the brink of destruction, urging me to embrace virtue and moral rectitude. She expressed regret for her own choices and envied Emma's apparent respectability, reflecting on her own path of sin and infamy.

Our letters varied in tone as Helen's moods shifted, from love to jealousy to threats of vengeance. Despite the turmoil, we occasionally met at the theater, where I confessed my affection for Sophia and my desire to abandon my nefarious ways and marry responsibly. Helen's response ranged from skepticism to tears, but she ultimately expressed a desire for my well-being and reminisced about her lost chances for a better life.

Helen spoke of her enemies and her fears of a shortened life, hinting at potential dangers. She discussed her financial arrangements and her disillusionment with solitude and reflection. Our conversation delved into her desires for security and her doubts about finding peace away from the city. She asked for a hatchet, and we made plans to meet again, unaware of the tragic events that would follow on that fateful Saturday night.

Let me continue in an organized manner. On that fateful Saturday evening, I had agreed to meet Helen to retrieve my picture and letters, intending to burn them and end our personal connection. This marked my initial step towards reform, filling me with renewed hope that I could return to the path of moral righteousness from which I had strayed. I envisioned fulfilling my obligations in adulthood to God and humanity, seeking forgiveness from my Creator for the indiscretions of my youth, and ultimately finding peace and happiness.

Anticipating my liberation from the bondage Helen had imposed on me for two long years, I enjoyed a relaxing tea and made plans to ride out with fellow boarders the next morning. After ten o'clock, I prepared for my visit, wearing a cloak I kept for disguises. Initially planning to visit Helen early in the evening but not wanting to prolong the encounter, I parted ways with my companion (as he testified during the trial) and headed towards Clinton Hall. However, instead of risking recognition in my extravagant attire, I opted to visit an Oyster Cellar near the Park to pass the time, observing the activities of various groups until nine o'clock.

At that hour, I directed my steps towards Thomas Street, where I observed a man heavily wrapped, knocking at a door. Pausing to assess the situation, I heard the name *Frank Rivers* called, saw the stranger enter, and then the door closed, cutting off any further sounds. Realizing that Helen would likely be unavailable for some time, I decided to wander into the business district of the city, casually entering Mr. C's store. We engaged in social conversation, discussing various topics until the clock struck ten, signaling the store's impending closure. Taking my leave, I headed back towards Thomas Street.

Passing through the hall of a Chapel Street house occupied by respectable people of color, I caught a glimpse of light in Helen's chamber window and observed shadows moving inside. Helen's figure shielded me from view as I quietly slipped in unnoticed by all but one observer. Upon her arrival, Helen remarked on my nimble entrance, joking that I could steal an heiress with such agility. We then discussed the purpose of my visit; she handed over the picture but refused to part with the letters, insisting that I return for them later. When I expressed discontent with this arrangement, she became tense. Trying to defuse the situation, I requested champagne, picked up a book to hide my face, and lay down on the bed with my back turned towards the door.

Helen returned without the wine, as Mrs. Townsend had brought it up, driven by curiosity to see who was with Ellen. However, Helen took the wine from her upon entering and promptly shut the door, allowing Mrs. Townsend only a brief glimpse of the back of my head, leading her to identify me based on hearsay.

Helen and I shared a glass of wine and then sat by the dying fire, where I wrapped my cloak around her. We conversed quietly until past midnight, at which point Helen lit a candle for me, and I took the lamp to guide me downstairs. When I reached Mrs. Townsend's door and requested my freedom, I was denied. So, I left the lamp in the hall, slipped into the yard, climbed over three fences, and found an open door through which I passed into Chapel Street, making my way home. The Hall clock chimed one as I entered my boarding house.

I entered my bedroom cheerfully, placed the miniature in my bureau, and peacefully drifted into sleep until my roommate woke me to inquire about my return to bed. I replied that I had been asleep and drifted back into a restful state until awakened by legal authorities.

Upon being awakened by Mr. Brink, my initial fear was that my financial misdeeds had been uncovered by Mr. Hoxie, and Helen had exposed me to legal consequences. This fear rendered me passive and compliant until the accusation of murder was leveled against me. However, my innocence eventually reassured my kind employer, instilling hope for the future.

This narrative encompasses all I have to share about my past. Despite my youthful age, experience had bestowed wisdom upon me. Henceforth, I am determined to resist the temptations of the world and avoid being ensnared by the charms of a deceitful woman. If I had not visited Helen that fatal night, someone else would have been accused. The identity of the person who accused me of murder remains unknown to me. The blame was broadly attributed when Mr. Brink arrived, according to the watchmen's testimony. Mrs. Townsend's words hinted at a collective responsibility with the mention of "They" causing the death and setting the fire.

I was labeled as the singular perpetrator, despite being one among many. My cloak, wrapped around Helen when I left her house, became a piece of circumstantial evidence against me. However, I did not plan the murder days in advance, as suggested, but instead spent the critical night with Helen, where I gave her the hatchet in question.

Had I intended to harm, I could have simply reported the house and avoided direct involvement. The accusations against me were fueled by prejudice and baseless assumptions. Mr. Phoenix's decision not to call certain witnesses was based on the understanding that their testimony would not add substance to the trial. I am grateful to those who saw through the falsehoods and spared my life.

Moving forward, I choose to distance myself from refined society's temptations, where appearances often deceive. My reputation now rests upon time and circumstance, and I seek refuge in a place where my integrity and hard work can redeem me in the eyes of the world. I write this not to gratify my enemies but to declare my innocence to those who may still doubt.

This letter concludes my account, and I bid farewell as a changed man, resolved to learn from my mistakes and lead a life guided by virtue and wisdom.

Richard P. Robinson

Mr. Armstrong's Address to the Public in Defense of the Jury

Having thoroughly reviewed Mr. Robinson's account of the case, I obtained a printed copy of the trial from New York to assess the basis for the public outcry against Richard, as well as the criticisms directed at the Jury, State's Attorney, and the many witnesses who supported him.

Upon examining all sworn testimonies and events presented in court, I firmly assert that there is no evidence to support any charges against Richard P. Robinson. Mrs. Townsend's testimony only confirms that someone resembling Richard was in Helen's room, reading around ten-thirty at night. Additionally, between two and three in the morning, Helen's lamp was found extinguished in the hall, and her bedclothes were on fire. Rather than waking Helen, Mrs. Townsend called for the city watch to put out the flames and protect her belongings. This summarizes the key points of the principal witness's testimony.

The first watchman to enter the scene stated that he encountered one man and two women at Helen's room door, who were allowed to escape without being searched or noticed much. Upon discovering Helen dead amidst the flames with a head wound, Mrs. Townsend exclaimed, "Oh! They have murdered her and set fire to the house!" The question arises: who was the "THEY" Mrs. Townsend referred to? Was it the man and woman who escaped during the chaos? Furthermore, one of the girls allegedly claimed to know the murderer's identity and intended to reveal it later. However, she was reported dead by the trial, and another man who had been in the house that night poisoned himself shortly after Helen's death, following a rumored trip to Boston. These circumstances suggest the involvement of someone, but not Richard P. Robinson. If the Jury adhered to their oath, they could not convict him, as there was no evidence supporting his guilt or even a reasonable accusation.

Mrs. Townsend's residence was extensive and housed some of society's most morally corrupt individuals. It is reasonable to assume that Helen Jewett's possessions in her chamber, including valuable items like a gold watch, trinkets, clothes, and money, could have tempted one of the immoral residents or visitors to commit the crime, especially since suspicion had not fallen on anyone specific.

During the trial, a witness described Helen Jewett as one of the best-dressed women frequenting the third tier of boxes at the Park Theater, mentioning her valuable possessions. This wealth could have enticed someone from the brothel to commit the crime and then deflect blame onto an innocent member of the community, whom the brothel's inhabitants already harbored animosity towards.

Regarding the accusations against Richard, it's unclear how much influence these motives had, if any. Robbery, jealousy, self-defense, or suspicion could have been underlying motives for the murder. Mrs. Townsend would likely not want to lose such a profitable tenant, which adds complexity to the case.

The whereabouts of Helen's valuables remain a mystery. If she had no relatives, the state or city would inherit them, necessitating transparent accounting to the public.

Criticism has been directed at Mr. Phoenix for not presenting all house inhabitants in court. However, given their escape at dawn and the chaotic situation, their testimonies may not have significantly impacted the trial's outcome. Mr. Furlough's testimony primarily disproved Richard's presence in the house at the time Mrs. Townsend claimed. As a juryman, one must prioritize the testimonies of reputable community members. It's incredulous to suggest that Mr. Furlough or other honorable figures involved would perjure themselves or induce others to do so. The notion is baseless and reflects poorly on the proceedings, which have unfairly tarnished a young man's reputation and brought distress to his family.

With hopes that justice prevails despite the press's persecution, I join with all decent individuals, especially parents and the jury who spared Richard's life, in praying for a fair resolution.

Sincerely,

Thomas Armstrong

The Court's Finale

It is not necessary to tire the reader with a report of the trial which lasted five days. Popular feeling had at first been rather in favor of the prisoner, but the developments of the trial caused a revulsion of feeling, and notwithstanding his acquittal, he stood branded as a murderer in the opinion of his fellow citizens.

Mr. Ogden Hoffman, who appeared for the defense, commenced by deploring the disadvantages under which the counsel for the prisoner labored, as compared with the prosecution, in the procuration of witnesses, and with great ingenuity assumed that the paucity of his testimony would be rather the result of artificial obstacles in his way, than the fact that there was no evidence in the existence in his behalf.

The crafty lawyer endeavored to arouse sympathy by repeatedly referring to his client as *this boy*! All that money could accomplish, in the way of bribery and otherwise, was done for Robinson. The grocer, previously referred to, made an oath to establish the alibi, and shortly afterward committed SUICIDE! He was evidently but a base hireling, and met his just desert in a watery grave of his own choosing, driven no doubt to his own taking off by the gnawing conscience of a guilty man. The district attorney, after regretting that some witnesses, for whom he had sent, had not been captured and brought in, reluctantly consented that the evidence on both sides should be closed. The witnesses who had thus failed the prosecution were the colored women who had seen Robinson escape by the cellar door into the street, after the commission of the murder. They had kept out of the way at the instigation of Gray and other of the prisoner's agents, and it was owing to this excellently managed portion of the business that his counsel was enabled to make a show for his defense.

Thus then to the amazement of the court and spectators the prisoner at the bar was pronounced *NOT GUILTY!*

The trial over, the extreme indignation of the community naturally alarmed the young murderer and gave uneasiness to his supporters, and when the leading journal denounced the verdict, some even went so far as to suggest that the accused should be tried for a separate offense of arson, considered their protege in absolute danger. Robinson thereupon bade farewell to the region of his crimes. Like Cain, his execrable prototype, he fled into the shadows of an unknown exile, with nothing behind him in the shape of recollection but universal detestation and the public's curse!

Helen Tells Her Story

As I sit here with my MacBook Air on my lap, I feel Helen's spirit standing next to me. An icy cool chill runs up and down the left side of my body and the hairs on my skin stand straight up. "Hello," she says, "My name is Helen, but you can call me Dorcas. I have been waiting a long time for someone on your side of the veil to share my story with. For my peace of mind, I need to reveal the identity of my murderer. Please pay close attention to what I say and show you. As soon as you publish my story, I can finally be at rest. So let's get started."

Almost immediately, a vision of two women standing and facing one another started to unfold. The much younger blonde-haired woman, who could have been around the age of sixteen, was upset and crying, The black-haired woman, who was also young, but appeared to be somewhat older than the blonde, stood with her arms folded. She maintained an air of dignity and remained calm and composed as the younger woman confronted her. "Helen, how could you! You know I love him and we have plans to be married! Why did you seduce him? Then, she slapped Helen on the face, turned around, and walked out of the room sobbing violently with her face in her hands. I heard Helen say loudly but calmly as the younger woman walked out, "Emma, I am so sorry. Our relationship happened long before you two met. He means nothing to me. I want you and Richard to be very happy. I promise to leave, and you will never have to see me again. Please don't throw away your relationship with Richard. You must go through with the marriage."

The vision changes and I see Helen standing in a bedroom. There are opened carpet bags and trunks spread out over a large four-poster bed. The walls of this room are painted light blue and there are many windows with sunlight streaming brightly through each one of them. This space emanates joy, wholesomeness, and comfort. I could feel Helen's love for this room and she didn't want to leave, but she had no choice. She could not let the situation get any worse with Emma.

The vision continues to play out like a movie and in the next scene, I see men loading Helen's luggage onto the back of a large stagecoach. After the luggage is loaded, Helen boards the coach and appears to be its only customer. The streets seemed very congested and busy on this day; however, the ride was a short distance. I perceive that the new boarding house was only a few short blocks away from the one she left.

The scene shifted, and I saw a brown-haired man arrive at the front door of a large white house. I heard the name Richard Robinson and could feel his masked anger. Rosina greeted him and summoned Helen from the parlor. As they ascended the stairs together, I sensed a shadowy black and red aura clinging to Robinson, an ominous sign of what was to come.

As the vision evolved I heard Helen say, "I was with Richard Robinson on the night I died. We spent most of our time together in my room where we enjoyed conversation and a bottle of champagne to celebrate his upcoming nuptials with Emma. I had promised myself that I would no longer be intimate with Richard, but one thing led to another and before I knew it we were indulging in a little sensual delight. Afterward, we fell asleep in each other's arms. We always had an understanding that he was never to spend the entire night in my room; he had to leave before the first morning light, and this night was no different. So, when he got out of bed, I assumed he was just leaving as usual and chose to continue my slumber. The next thing I remember is that I saw a flash of light and was standing beside my bed looking down on my body. I noticed that my head was bloody and had a big hole in it. I wondered if I was having a nightmare and tried to wake myself up, but I couldn't. I watched as Richard dowsed my body with oil from the lamp. Then he walked over to the mantelpiece, pulled out a long stem match from the matchbox, struck it on the side of the fireplace grate, and flung it onto my bed.

I couldn't understand why he would do this, and then it occurred to me that he came to the house for only one reason—to kill me. He was avenging the loss of his relationship with Emma. He lied when he said that he came over to let me know everything was okay and that he and Emma were going ahead with their wedding plans. He suggested a champagne toast as a way to lure me into his dubious plan. As soon I laid eyes on him from the parlor room, I remembered the pledge I made to myself—to refuse to see him again. But, he said he urgently needed to talk to me and that we should go to my room.

The visions continued as I watched each scene as if through Helen's eyes. I saw Robinson nimbly descend the stairs with the lamp from Helen's room to illuminate his way. He started towards the front door and realized he couldn't go out that way because the night watchmen would see him. He turned back around and as he passed the front parlor, he placed the lamp on a nearby table and quickly headed for the back door. He quietly escaped through the back door, cleared a short set of steps off the porch, and mounted a wooden fence about ten yards to his right. Although his body cleared the fence, his cloak became caught between two slats, ripping the hatchet from the tassel inside his garment. It fell to the grassy ground, the blood-stained metal reflecting the night's bright moonlight. I continued to watch as he scaled one fence after another making his way down several blocks before crossing the street and disappearing completely from my sight into the velvety darkness.

My attention returned to the house which fell silent as the fire ravaged Helen's body and consumed the bed and draperies of a nearby window. I watched as Rosina let in another visitor. On her way back she noticed that a lamp belonging to Helen was lit and in the parlor. She pondered for a moment why the lamp would be in the parlor and not in Helen's room. With keys and the lamp in hand, Rosina approached Helen's room. As she unlocked the door, a rush of smoke billowed out, practically suffocating her. The bed was ablaze. She ran downstairs crying out to everyone that Helen's room was on fire. Upon reaching the front door, she screamed for help, alerting the night watchmen standing nearby.

As the vision continued, I looked on as several men worked to get a hose connected to a fire hydrant located across the street while two other men retrieved a wooden ladder from a nearby wagon and placed it against the front of the house at the window that was spewing smoke. Another man grabbed the end of the hose and scurried up the ladder. Just inside the window, the fireman directed the forceful flow of water onto the flames that were issuing from the bed and curtains. Within a matter of minutes, the fire was extinguished revealing Helen's lifeless body lying on her back, her left side charred beyond recognition.

I could read the thoughts that were running through the minds of the watchmen standing around the room. They initially assumed that her death was by fire and smoke. However, as one of the watchmen approached the bed, he noticed something more sinister—a deep, gaping gash to her head. I heard this man tell the other men that they had to get the jury coroner right away because the young lady had been murdered.

Once again the scene shifted and I found myself inside a courtroom. I watched from somewhere near the ceiling as a trial proceeded below. Sitting at the defense bench was Richard accompanied by two counselors. On the other bench sat three gentlemen, one of whom stood up and walked over to the witness stand. He was questioning a young African American woman. I couldn't make out what they were saying, but I knew that the testimony was not favorable for the prosecution. After she left the stand, the judge addressed the jury, then everyone proceeded out of the courtroom.

The vision continued as I remained in the empty courtroom. I'm not sure how much time elapsed before everyone filed back in. Nevertheless, as soon as everyone was seated, the judge asked the jury foreman if he had a verdict. The foreman nodded his head, stood up, and handed a small piece of paper to a clerk who walked it over to the judge.

The judge glanced at the piece of paper, turned to the jury foreman who was still standing, and asked, "Sir, what is your verdict?"

The silence was so great you could have heard a pin drop when the foreman announced: "We, the jury, find the defendant Not Guilty!"

The courtroom erupted into chaos with spectators and witnesses on the prosecutor's side shouting, "He's guilty, He's guilty and must be punished! Justice has not been served! We demand justice now!

Their demands fell on deaf ears as Richard Robinson was escorted out of the room by several deputies.

As the vision ended, I heard Helen say that although the jury's verdict of not guilty was rendered that day, the public's verdict of guilty was also rendered, and Richard P. Robinson was practically forced out of the city. She said that he made his way to Texas where he married, raised a family, and became a respected man in the community.

Before her voice faded away, she said, "Thank you for telling my story. I see the light and will cross over now. Richard is still in the astral realm because he is afraid of going to hell. Please reach out to him and help him cross over into the light. Let him know that people on your side of the veil know that he killed me, and they have forgiven him, I have forgiven him and so has God."

Later on the same day, I assumed a comfortable position in my recliner, centered myself and called out to Richard P. Robinson. Within a few moments, the face of a man with light brown hair and green eyes appeared within two inches of my face. I told him to back off.

He replied, "You back off! You called me; I didn't call you; what do you want?"

I told him, "I don't want anything. Helen asked me to help you cross over."

"Really?" he said, "That sneaky bitch! She just wants you to cross me over into hell!"

I said, "That's not true! She told me to tell you that she has forgiven you, people on earth have forgiven you, and most importantly God has forgiven you. She received forgiveness for her misdeeds in life and has crossed over into the loving light of the Creator. She wants the same for you too!"

"Look Madame Medium," he replied, "I am not crossing over, so just forget it! I don't need your help. I'll go when I'm ready!"

I ended the conversation by saying, "When you are tired of hanging out in your favorite haunts, let me know and I will show you how beautiful heaven is and help you cross over."

With this comment, he backed up, raised his astral hatchet, and hit me on the side of the head with it. Fortunately, because it was an astral hatchet, it just caused me to experience a momentary sharp pain, but that's it, no real damage was done. If he ever decides he's ready to cross over, he knows where to find me. I think he knows that I will not tolerate any abuse from him and that I have the power to force him over, whether it be heaven or hell. I don't ever expect to hear from him, and that's just fine with me!

~ 4 ~

CASE FILE #3: MARY CECILIA ROGERS-THE BEAUTIFUL CIGAR GIRL

Mary Cecilia Rogers
*Public Domain**The Cruel Murder of the Beautiful Cigar Girl***

Case Summary

Name of Deceased: Mary Cecilia Rogers

Date of Birth: circa 1820 or1821, no record has survived

Date of Death: between July 25th, and July 28th, 1841

Location: Hoboken, N. J.

Deceased Found by: fishermen setting their nets off Castle Point near the shore, not far from Sybil's Cave

Relationship to the Deceased: None

Complainant: John Anderson filed a complaint with the New York police department

Relationship to the Deceased: Previous employer at a cigar shop

Witnesses: None

Estimated Time of Death: Sometime between July 25th and July 28th when her body was discovered

Position of Body: Floating in the Hudson River

Wounds: Mutilation of the face, abrasions to the neck and wrists

Autopsy Findings: Dr. Richard Cook reported that Mary had been cruelly assaulted by one or more men. Before the assault, she was a *good girl* (virgin).

Disposition: Cold Case, Never Solved

Background Informant Source: Duke, T. (1920). *The Mysterious Murder of Cigar Girl Mary Rogers, 1841.* Celebrate Criminal Cases of America.

Background on the Murder of Mary Cecilia Rogers

Mary Cecilia Rogers was a girl of twenty-one, whose beauty must have been more than passing, although the only picture of her I have found evidently fails to reflect all of her charms in this respect. Her bright smile, which is said to have been irresistible, perhaps was difficult to recapture. It was this smile that had caught the eye of John Anderson, a canny tobacconist, a few years before. Sensing its irresistibility, and, incidentally, translating it into dollars and cents, he had placed the girl behind the cigar counter in his shop on the corner of Broadway and Thomas Street, and with gratifying results. Business picked up immediately. Almost any man is a fool for a pretty face, as the saying goes, and Mr. Anderson's cigars were probably as good as the next shop's, where a none-too-handsome old gentleman with a straggly beard was his won salesman.

The beautiful cigar girl soon became something of a town character. It is reported that Mr. Fitz-Greene Halleck wrote a poem to her loveliness. Mr. Poe's subsequent interest in her demise may be traced partly to the fact that he had been one of her admiring customers. Mr. Janes Fenimore Cooper often took a few moments from Elles, as the saying goes, to chat with her, and even Mr. Washington Irving, who was on his next to last legs, hobbled in now and again to buy a cigar that perhaps he did not really need.

These, however, were just the celebrities. They were not alone among her admirers by any means. The gamblers who loafed on the Broadway corners until time to gather at the faro table knew her, and the gay blades of an increasing conventional society, who were just beginning to go in for white gloves and such, were numbered, too, among her casual friends. Let it be said now, as it was then, that she knew how to handle them all. She had a pleasant word for everyone but it didn't go beyond that. It was Mr. Anderson who walked home with her every night, for she and her mother had rooms at her employer's house. Apparently, she did not permit romance to raise its ugly head in the cigar business.

And then one day she was gone. She had left Mr. Anderson's house on an errand and had failed to return. Her mother was frankly worried and Mr. Anderson, although he took her place at the counter with a commercially cheery smile, was obviously disturbed. In a week she was back, with the explanation that she had felt tired and had gone to the country to rest with some relatives.

Her mother evidently accepted this explanation and so did Mr. Anderson. But with the Broadway boys, it was as it would be now. She was too pretty to escape rumors. There were many of them. The most persistent was that she had gone off for a week with a handsome naval officer. There were some, too, who expressed the belief that the whole business had been arranged with the connivance of Mr. Anderson to attract attention to his cigar store.

However, if it was what we might call today a publicity stunt, it was hardly worth the effort on the part of Mr. Anderson, for within a few weeks after her return she left his employ for good. It was explained that Mary's brother who had gone to sea several years before had made a strike of some kind in South America and had come back with his pockets filled with gold. He bought his mother a house at 126 Nassau Street, which she converted into a boarding house. She was old and infirm, and it was necessary for Mary to help her in this new undertaking. So Mr. Anderson's cigars lost Mary along with some business.

Once the girl and her mother had started upon this new venture the brother went off to sea again and Mary settled down to a simpler life running the boarding house with her mother. Alfred Crommelin, a rather attractive young man was one of their first boarders. He was more interested in Mary than in the table set by Mrs. Rogers. He did not conceal his regard for her. But Mary evidently did not return his affections. She was pleasant enough to him but that was not enough. Mr. Crommelin was a sensitive soul. If he could not be dear to Mary as well as near, he did not want to be near. So he moved away. He couldn't go, however, without his little scene. When he said his farewell he told the girl, possibly in a theatrical little speech which he had rehearsed before his mirror, that if she ever changed her mind or if she ever was in trouble and needed him she should come to him. And, for good measure, he told her mother, too.

Among the boarders was Daniel Payne. Just why Mary, with all the beaux of the town to choose from, should have been attracted to

Mr. Payne is something of a mystery. It wasn't a question of money, for he had very little. He was a cork cutter by trade but he evidently had little liking for work and wasn't steady at it. He much preferred his drinking, at which he had developed no little efficiency. When Mary walked out, which was seldom, it was with Payne. It subsequently developed that she was never known to leave the house with anyone else as an escort. In fact, it was reported that she had pledged herself to marry him, and in those conventional days a maid, once betrothed, was rarely if ever, seen in public with any man but her fiancé.

On Sunday morning, July 25th, Mary knocked at Payne's door and told him that she was going to the home of her cousin, Mrs. Downing, in Jane Street. There was nothing unusual in the announcement. She had made the call many times. Paynes was shaving at the moment and, without leaving his mirror, called out from the corner of his mouth that he would, as usual, see the stage that brought her back to Broadway and Ann Street at about seven o'clock that evening.

It turned out to be a miserably torrid summer day, "the hottest," according to Monday's Herald, "we have ever experienced," wherever that was, and one elderly gentleman, who evidently couldn't find it, was stricken with coup de soleil, which would be sunstroke to you. Payne spent the long afternoon meandering about the lower part of the city, stopping here and there for a drink.

When evening came on there were unmistakable signs of an impending, and welcome, storm. As seven o'clock approached, Payne came to the conclusion that Mary would not even venture from her cousin's tight roof into the ominous beclouded calm and so did not make an effort to meet the stage as he had promised.

Shortly before nine o'clock the deluge came, with thunder and lightning for good measure, and feeling certain now that Mary would spend the night at her cousin's he went to bed. She had not returned when he left the house in the morning but he thought little of that. When, however, he came back to dinner at noon and found her still missing, he was concerned and set out for Mrs. Downing's. He was met at the front door with the news that she had not been there at all!

Alarmed by this time he began a search for her. There were few enough places she might be and she was at none of these. Her mother, infirm, could not participate in the search and could offer little assistance in the way of advice. When the day was spent and there was no trace of her, Payne placed an advertisement in the Sun, the most widely read of the penny papers, reporting her disappearance, and asking for any information that anyone might have as to her whereabouts.

Alfred Crommelin read the advertisement the next day. He recalled that on Saturday when he had returned from dinner he had found on the slate which was posted outside his office door for messages the name of Mary's mother, written in Mary's handwriting. In the keyhole, there was a rose. This sentimental gesture might have been expected to arouse the whilom swain, but he was still smoldering under the earlier rebuff and did nothing about it. But when he saw the advertisement he became conscience-stricken, perhaps with the thought that Mary had sought his aid in trouble, and began his own search for her.

It took him on Wednesday morning to Hoboken, which was not so strange as it seems to those of you who know the Hoboken of today. In the 1840's this New Jersey faubourg was "beautiful, rosy Hoboken, a spot of sylvan loveliness, which afforded a magnificent view of the city and the bay. Its "Elysian Fields" had charming lanes and shady arbors. There were picnic grounds and refined amusements and there were public houses where a man could sip his sherry and cobbler while a maid nibbled at an ice. Steamboats took harried New Yorkers to its shore on a Sunday and there they whiled away an idle day.

Mr. Crommelin, it seems, suspected that Mary might have decided to give herself a good time, although he probably was a little shocked at the thought of her having gone to Hoboken unescorted.

He had made a few inquiries for her here and there when he was attracted by a commotion on the shore near Sybil's Cave, a cool spot hewn out of the solid rock where the Sunday throngs bought spring water for a penny a glass and beer at a little more.

Hurrying to the scene Mr. Crommelin found three men in a boat, towing ashore the body of a young girl which they had found floating in the river. The face was mutilated beyond recognition, but the little blue dress and the bonnet with its ribbons still tied and hanging loose about her neck told Mr. Crommelin at once that it was Mary. That she had been murdered there was no question. A strip of lace torn from an underskirt was tied about her neck and there were cords about her wrists. It was again a beastly hot day and it was considered important that all that remained of Mary should be buried as soon as possible, so they carried her into the little town of Hoboken and held a hasty autopsy. Crommelin identified her. Dr. Richard Cook examined her and reported that she had been "cruelly assaulted" by one or more men and that prior to that assault she had been what is known as "a good girl." There were the usual official formalities, hastily attended to, and, these over, her body was buried in Hoboken. Mr. Crommelin hurried back to Mary's mother with a flower from her hat and a strip of her pantalettes from which his identification was confirmed with tears and then more tears.

Here, then, was New York's third great murder mystery with a lovely young girl as its victim and the twin talking of little else. Who killed Mary Rogers? That was the question that everyone asked of everyone else. And it would seem, from all that happened subsequently, that everyone but the police sought the answer.

At first, there arose the question of jurisdiction. The minions of New York declared that Mary Roger had been killed in New Jersey and that the solution to her murder was up to the officials of that state. Their answer was that Mary Roger had been slain in New York and her body thrown into the river to float to the Jersey shore. But even when the newspaper of New York pointed out, with bitter emphasis, that Mary Rogers was a resident of New York and that, no matter where the crimes were actually committed, the law under which she had lived should all that was possible to avenge her, there was little activity.

New York's police system, at the moment, was in a sad state that did not make for efficiency. Fundamentally, the city was still under the somewhat dubious protection of the leather-heads who walked the streets at night crying out the hour so lustily as to warn any caitiffs that might be engaged in dirty work of their approach. To these night watchmen had been added a day force of "roundsmen," who were detectives in that they wore no helmets to permit their ready identification but who were utterly unschooled in the science of criminology. They were, for the most part, recited from the ranks of unsuccessful stevedores, cartmen, porters, and laborers.

The watchmen were woefully underpaid, receiving only a little more than $1 a night, and the roundsmen were not paid at all, being dependent upon the fees, which they received for serving papers and the rewards they might collect from citizens who sought to recover stolen property. Thus many of them had formed alliances with thieves. The partnerships worked in this way: the criminal would, under the protection of the officer, commit a robbery, the victim would offer a reward for the return of the loot, and the roundsman would return it and divide the reward with the thief. It didn't make for law and order.

Under this system, murder was a crime that did not interest the police to any great extent. So when the body of Mary Rogers was found the roundsmen shrugged their shoulders. They would have had to pay their own expenses in any investigation they undertook. A reward might have spurred them but the governors of New Jersey and New York showed no disposition to offer one. Weeks later a committee of citizens, at an indignation meeting, subscribed $500 for the apprehension of the murderer, and Governor Seward, thus shamed, offered a state reward of $750, but it was too late then to do much good.

From the start, the solution was left largely to idle tongues and they made the most of it. If there was no one to ferret out real clues there were plenty to start false ones. The first of these was a report, published at the time of the discovery of the body, that upon leaving her home that scorching Sunday morning Mary had met "a young man with whom she apparently was acquainted" at Theater Alley, a lane branching off Ann Street near Broadway which once led to the stage door of the Park Theater, and had proceeded with hime toward Barclay Street as if to go to Hoboken. Where this report started is a complete mystery, for no one was ever found who had seen such a meeting.

Came then a Mrs. Loss, of Hoboken with a story that Mary and a beau had stopped on Sunday afternoon at her refreshment house for a lemonade and had wandered into the shady lanes of the Elysian Fields. Came also a Mr. Adams, a stage driver, with the story that he had picked up Mary and a tall dark man at the Bull's Head ferry and driven them to the pleasure grounds of Hoboken.

Came also two gentlemen who had been strolling on the Hoboken shore that Sunday afternoon when a rowboat containing six young men and the beautiful cigar girl had pulled up. All had alighted and the girl had skipped merrily into the woods with her plenteous escort. A moment later another rowboat containing three young men had drawn up. These three had asked the two gentlemen whether they had seen a girl and six men. They replied that they had and that they had gone into the woods. Had the girl gone willingly? The three wanted to know. She had. Whereupon, according to one of the gentlemen, the three had followed the seven into the woods. However, according to the other, the three had got back into their rowboat and set off again for the New York side. For all that came of it, it didn't make much difference which was right.

There were theories of jealousy, but although there were many who might have envied Payne his place in the affections of the erstwhile, saleslady of cigars there was none who had betrayed a passion so violent that it might turn from love to hate and murder.

There were theories of robbery, too, for Mary's rings were gone, but they were pitiful little trinkets worth only a few dollars at most.

There were stories that the girl had been a victim of one of the groups of young roisterers who often, on Sunday afternoons, had annoyed young ladies at the beaches by trying to peek into their bathhouses. An anonymous pamphlet which was given wide circulation, at a penny a copy, openly accused a group of young gamblers who made a Broadway corner near Mr. Anderson's cigar store their hangout and addressed flip remarks to any girl who passed by unescorted.

The darkest of all the explanations was based upon an unverified story that Mary was last seen on Greenwich Street near the shadowy establishment of Mme. Restell.

This would have given the lie to Dr. Cook's optimistic theory of the girl's good name, for Mme. Restell's shuttered residence was called the mansion built on baby skulls and she was known to the police, and many as a fashionable but not eternally ambitious lady, as an abortionist. All of these suspicions are vague at best and go from lip to lip only to disappear into the vapor of a great buzz of conversation. There were others less nebulous who were half-heartedly run to earth by indifferent police. Naturally, the first substantial shadow fell on Payne. The newspapers decided he had behaved in an unloverlike manner. But Payne, a little the worse for a consoling sup, appeared at the office of the policed justice with a complete accounting for every moment of the dreadful day. Crommelin, the victim of similar whispers, was also able to clear himself with a complete alibi.

When, as a result of public demand, the body of May was exhumed and brought back to lie for days in the Death House in New York, it was discovered that a strip of skirt had been tied about her waits evidently to aid the murdered in throwing her body into the river and that this was tied in a sailor's knot. The police went snooping about the waterfront and brought in one William Kukuck, a sailor from North Carolina, who had known Mary a year before. It was said that there were stains on his trousers that might be blood and that he had been in a great hurry to get aboard his ship late the night of July 25th. But he was held only for a day and satisfied the authorities that he had not seen the girl since June.

There was another great flurry when it was found that a Mr. Joseph M. Morse, a wood engraver of 129 Nassau Street, not far from Mary's home, had disappeared the morning the body was discovered after appearing at his home in a great fright and giving his wife a good beating. He had been seen on the street that Sunday afternoon with a young girl, which did not make things any better for him.

He was traced to a little town near Worcester, Mass., where he was found living under an assumed name. In his pocket was a letter from one of his clerks advising him to shave off his elegant black whiskers and to stay away as long as possible. When he was led trembling back to town the indignant citizenry was prepared to make a victim of him. Mr. Morse admitted that he had been out with a young lady on the Sunday in question and that she had fled the city because he believed that young lady to be Mary Rogers.

But he was sure he had not murdered her. He had taken her to Staten Island and, by manipulating his watch, caused her to miss the last ferry back. Then he had taken her to a hotel. But she had resisted his advances and he had left her the next morning peevish with frustration. A likely story! But before a noose could be made officially for the gentleman's neck the girl herself came forward to confirm the account as given by Mr. Morse and to prove that she wasn't Mary Rogers. She was more than a little proud of herself for having resisted his attentions. Reluctantly the authorities let their victim go and Mr. Morse was no worse for the experience except that it took him some weeks to square himself with his wife and even longer to grow a new set of whiskers.

And so went each clue to the murder of Mary Roger. In late September two sons of Mrs. Loss, out gathering sassafras bark, came upon a clearing in the woods and found there signs of a struggle and, under heavy mildew, a wild scarf, a white petticoat, and a parasol, and a linen handkerchief with the initials M. R. The were all identified as having belonged to the murdered girl, but if this was the spot of the actual murder it was too late to trace even the footprints that might have led from it.

In this very thicket some two weeks later, the body of Daniel Payne. It was thought at first that he had taken his own life and that a guilty conscience had driven him to it. But Payne's alibi held as firmly in death as it had in life, and a medical examination showed that if he had committed suicide it was through the indirect method of drinking himself into this grassy grave he chose. From the moment his fiancee had been taken from him he had haunted the public houses, staggering out each night filled with the run and self-pity.

Many years later when Mme. Restell decided to end her harassed life by committing suicide in her expensive bathtub, the case was revived again by the newspapers and the gossipers, and the blame for the murder was conveniently placed upon her cold shoulders, but again without proof. Still later John Anderson, the cigar site man, departed this life at a ripe old age. His relatives told their friends that he had known who murdered Mary Rogers. But when the police looked into it they found that Mr. Anderson got his information from Mary's ghost, which had come to him one night and told him all about how she was murdered— nice little bedtime story. Naturally, such a message was confidential and he couldn't repeat it. Also, in his late eighties, Mr. Anderson was a trifle senile. Perhaps there were other stories, too. When a murder is unsolved, officially, it is usually solved unofficially by every idle imagination. There must have been hundreds of versions that did not even get the dignity of type and were not handed down as lore. But they came to nothing, of course. Who killed Mary Rogers was a burning question in 1841. One that wouldn't be answered until the twenty-first century. Had the police listened to Mr. Anderson, who by the way I am told was a Medium, the murderers would have been revealed a long time ago. Once again Mary tells her story. This time it will go to print. I'll make sure of that!

Mary Tells Her Story

No sooner had I sat down at my laptop with the intent of communicating with the spirit of Mary than she appeared to me as a full spectral apparition in a vision. Long dark curls cascaded from underneath her blue bonnet. Her big blue eyes glittered as she smiled at me and said:

> I have been waiting so long for another chance to tell my story. My dear friend Mr. Anderson, who, like you, could communicate with spirits, tried to relay my message, but no one believed him. They thought he was confused and wouldn't listen. Now, I am depending on you to let people know what really happened to me so I can find peace and cross over. I need everyone to understand that my behavior may not have always been ladylike, but I did nothing to deserve the brutal murder I endured.
>
> I was innocent of any impropriety on the day I was murdered. My only sin was that I enjoyed the attention I received from men. I liked being treated special, like a lady. Also, I suppose I was naive to believe the lies I was told by the six men who approached me and called themselves sailors. They were very complimentary of me and seemed to be very nice. They asked me why such a pretty girl was hanging around the docks, and I told them I was waiting for my beau, Robert, who was a Naval Officer. One of the sailors said, 'Oh! You're the one Robert asked us to escort. His ship arrived an hour ago, and he went to the jewelry store to buy a ring for you. It's supposed to be a secret, but he wants to propose to you in the Elysian Fields. He asked us to take you there to await his arrival, so we best get going.

As the vision continued, I witnessed several men helping Mary step down into what appeared to be a large rowboat. The so-called sailors laughed and passed around a bottle of whiskey while they flattered and flirted with Mary. This scene continued for a while until they reached the shore of Hoboken. They exited the boat one by one and ran, skipping down a sandy path towards the woods. I could feel Mary's excitement at the prospect of seeing her Naval officer. Her head and heart swirled together in anticipation of a possible engagement proposal.

My vision switched to the scene of a handsome dark-haired man dressed as a naval officer, who I assumed to be Robert, standing on a shipping dock looking for the beautiful cigar girl. After what I perceived as an hour of waiting, he became restless and started walking about, asking sailors who were standing about if they had seen a woman fitting Mary's description. He asked several men before stumbling across a couple of sailors who said they saw a woman fitting Mary's description leaving the dock with several men about an hour earlier. One of the two men said he overheard them talking about the Elysian Fields of Hoboken. Robert thanked the two men and mumbled something about going to find her. The two sailors offered to go with Robert, stating that the group of men she went off with looked like hooligans, and it might be a good idea for them to accompany him in case there was trouble.

This scene morphed into the next with the three men leaving their boat. They saw a couple of fishermen repairing their nets on the beach and asked them if they had seen a woman fitting Mary's description. The men said they had seen a very beautiful woman merrily skipping along with a group of thugs and pointed to the sandy path leading to the woods. They said they couldn't understand why such a beautiful lady would be with such rugged-looking thugs.

The three men headed for the path, with Robert leading the way. They walked quietly and briskly, hoping to catch Mary and her thugs by surprise. As they approached a clearing in the woods, they heard laughter. Following the laughter, they found Mary sitting on the lap of one of the so-called sailors. They stood quietly behind a bush and watched for several minutes as Mary appeared to be flirting with the men. I could feel the disgust rising in Robert. As he turned to walk away, his jacket caught a large branch on the bush, causing it to shake. One of the thugs sitting on a log close to the bush heard the rustle of movement. He stood up and ran towards the bush, screaming, 'Who's there?' Mary followed behind the man until they reached the path beyond the bush. The other men ran up from behind to investigate the happenings. Mary yelled out to Robert and started to run after him; however, the thugs surrounded them and escorted her back to the clearing. Mary tried once again to run after Robert, but one of the thugs threw her down on the ground, ripped the lace hem off her underskirt, and used part of it to gag her mouth. Mary tried to get up, but the thug threw her to the ground again. Another thug took the remnants of the lacy hem and ripped it into several pieces. He used these pieces to tie her wrists to the branches of a large bush while the other thug held Mary down. Mary fought to no avail. Finally, she gave up the struggle and just cried.

With her wrists tied to the tree, the thug who was holding her down pulled off her pantaloons and tossed them to the side. He mounted Mary, and after pulling out his disgusting little manhood, sexually assaulted her. As tears rolled down her face, I heard him say, 'Stop crying, you wench, or I'll give you the beating you deserve!' Mary continued to sob uncontrollably. As promised, the thug beat her in the head until she lost consciousness.

One by one, they took their turns violating her. As soon as they finished the first round, they started a second one. When they had finished the second round, the last thug to rape her said, 'She's not breathing; I think she might be dead.' He got off of her and, while putting his stuff back in his pants, he kicked her in the ribs as hard as he could and said, 'Move, you whore!' Mary didn't respond, not even with a grimace. The group surrounded her and, upon close observation, concluded that she was definitely dead.

The youngest looking of the group panicked and started pacing around, crying, 'Oh my God; we're gonna hang for this!' One of the scruffier older-looking thugs replied, 'Shut up, you idiot! Nobody is gonna hang. We'll wait until it's dark and put her body in the river. No one will ever be the wiser. How are they gonna know it's us?' The younger man became silent and sat down on a log.

The afternoon sun morphed into darkness as gray clouds gathered and lightning streaked across the sky. Rain fell in torrents as the group sat in their little clearing off the main path. No one said a word, not because they had nothing to say, but because they were trying to hide their deed from passersby. As soon as the sun had dipped below the horizon, and darkness set in, one of the thugs, out of fear that Mary might not be dead, tied a piece of lace around her neck and used it to strangle her. They used the ribbon tied around her wrists to drag her body along the path she had so merrily skipped along earlier that day. As expected, the beach was empty when they reached it. They hurriedly ran to their boat, dragging Mary's body behind them. Four of them heaved Mary's body over the side of the rowboat while the other two looked around for a rock they could use to try and sink her body. It didn't take them long to find a rock big enough to do the job but light enough to carry. They jumped into the boat where the other thugs were waiting and took off, rowing in the opposite direction of New York. They continued until they came upon an isolated area by the river where the water was deep. There, they tied the rope around the rock using a clove hitch knot and then tied it around Mary's waist with the same knot. Then they heaved Mary's body over the side of the boat and quickly threw the rock into the water with her. It was still raining as they turned and rowed the boat back up the river towards New York. (As an interesting side note: I write what I see and hear in my visions without making any judgments. (After writing this section, I researched the clove hitch knot and discovered that it was used to secure a dock line to a piling. Clove knots can unexpectedly work free as a boat moves around the dock driven by the current. This explains why Mary's body floated up to the top of the water. The rope remained around her waist, but the rock was at the bottom of the river. Obviously, the rope was not securely tied around the rock, and it worked itself free by the rocking of Mary's body by the strong current of the Hudson River.)

It had stopped raining when they returned to New York and docked the rowboat. I watched as they ran from the rowboat to board a medium-sized steamboat. Once aboard they went their own way and never again spoke of the beautiful cigar girl.

When this vision ended, I heard Mary say: 'Those devils got away with my murder. One of them was brought in by the New York police, but they let him go 'cause they didn't have enough proof that he was guilty."

I asked Mary if she knew the names of the thugs who murdered her, and she replied, "I remember the names: James R., William K., John S., and George W. I don't know the names of them all. William is the one who killed me. I am not looking to blame anyone for my death. I just need everyone to know that I was a good girl!"

My Psychic Impression of Mary Cecilia Rogers

I perceive that Mary was an adventurous soul who loved the outdoors, the smell of fragrant bushes and flowers, and the feel of sunshine on her face. She enjoyed exploring the unknown and loved to take hikes through the woods as well as the city streets. Mary was a high-spirited and vivacious young woman who enjoyed the playful exchange of family, friends, and customers. Her lively and cheerful behavior could have been perceived as flirting by many of her male cigar customers and acquaintances. Unfortunately for her, the majority of the men she was exposed to fell far below her standard of decency and moral character. She was a beautiful woman and could have had her choice of any well-to-do husband long before Robert appeared on the scene. I feel that she chose to identify with men of low standards and meager prospects because she believed that was her station in life, that a woman of her class could not aspire to anything better. Nevertheless, her story carries a strong message for women everywhere. As I wrote the last sentence, I heard Mary's voice chime in and say:

> Tell the women in your world that they need to see their self-worth. It's important for them not to allow men to take advantage of, or violate them in any manner. Women are precious gems deserving to be polished and cherished. Above all, be wise and discerning women. I paid a high price for being a naive and silly young woman. I suppose I was a product of my time. I have waited a long time for someone to tell my story. Thank you for publishing it! It saddens me that no one believed Mr. Anderson, but I know they'll believe you. It's time for me to cross over now and be with my mother. My business is finished.

I feel Mary's energy pulling away, so I must close the session with her. I believe she has finally let go of the need to be heard. She is free!

~ 5 ~

CASE FILE #4: BLAS TRUJILLO-MURDER OF A KIND CIGAR MAKER

Blas Trujillos
Public Domain

Case Summary

Name of Deceased: Blas Trujillos

Date of Birth: February 3, 1841

Date of Death: August 11, 1900

Location: His body was discovered in his office at Blas Trujillo & Co. Block of 14th and 17th Streets, Ybor City, Tampa, FL.

Deceased Found by: Not mentioned in the press

Relationship to the Deceased: N/A

Complainant: Not mentioned in the press

Relationship to the Deceased: N/A

Witnesses: None

Estimated Time of Death: Afternoon of August 11, 1900

Positions of Body: On the floor, gun by his right hand

Wounds: Bullet through the roof of the mouth into the head

Blood Splatters: Not mentioned

Autopsy Findings: Not performed

Disposition: Closed Case, Never Investigated

Background Informant Source: Blas Trujillo Is A Suicide: Cigar Manufacturer Ends His Life With a Pistol Bullet. (1900, August 12). *The Tampa Tribune.*

Background on the Murder of Blas Trujillos

From the late 1800s to the mid-1900s, Tampa, FL, was a hub of organized crime. The level of criminal activity was so severe that the federal government labeled Tampa as one of the most corrupt cities in the country.

Yesterday afternoon, Blas Trujillo, a renowned cigar manufacturer, was alone in his private office. Under the watchful eye of the All-Seeing, he placed a revolver against the roof of his mouth and fired, ending his life.

Trujillo had established his cigar manufacturing business in New York City thirty years ago. The factory was later moved to Key West and, in 1894, to Tampa. Trujillo relocated his business to Tampa along with other cigar manufacturers, drawn by Edward Manrara's generous offer of land and buildings. Since then, his business had generally thrived.

Blas Trujillo became famous for his cigars, such as El Blason, El Feniz, La Habanera, and La Belle Princesa Cigars, wherever Havana cigars were enjoyed. His impressive three-story factory, topped with a stately tower and a prominent clock, was one of the most complete in the country. It produced three million cigars annually, none of which were sold for less than ten cents or more than a dollar.

The news of Trujillo's death shocked Tampa, as well as cigar smokers and industry followers who associated his name with high-quality Havana cigars and business integrity.

Blas Trujillo's funeral took place on August 14, 1900, directed by Mrs. Theodore Grippers. It was a Masonic ceremony, as Trujillo was a Mystic Shriner and a high-ranking Mason. There was a large attendance at the funeral.

No clear motive for Trujillo's suicide has been found. Investigations revealed that the factory's affairs were in good order, and there were no typical reasons that might lead a man to take such a drastic step.

Blas Tells His Story

My husband and I had planned a day trip to Ybor City in Tampa, FL., to do some touring and take in the essence of this exciting little Latin city within a city. A few days before embarking on our trip, I had a dream one night in which I was transported to another time and place to witness the life and murder of a very kind and successful cigar manufacturer. The day after my dream, research for our planned trip put a name to the kindly man in my dream—Blas Trujillo.

In my dream, I saw the cobblestone streets of Ybor City bathed in a golden glow as if the sun itself held a secret, a secret that would soon unravel. Amid cigar smoke, stood a man, Blas Trujillo, a figure of charisma and resilience. He talked about how he had emerged from humble beginnings to become a giant in the cigar industry. He showed me his factory and said it was a testament to the ultimate craftsmanship of its time. I perceived the building as being a red brick structure with several stories. As I entered the front entrance of the first floor, I noticed several smaller rooms to the left-hand side of a large open space. This open space showcased shelves of many different types and qualities of boxed cigars. Somewhere near the rear of the room, I ascended the stairs to the second level. This level was an open space lined with wooden work tables and chairs. It was a place where countless souls found their livelihoods, souls who had, like Blas, ventured to these shores in search of a brighter future.

I perceive that Ybor City, a close-knit community rooted in cigar factories, flourished under Blas's benevolent influence. He saw not just the chance to make a name for himself, but also to offer a lifeline to those who had journeyed here, seeking a new and prosperous life. With unwavering dedication and a deep, almost mystical connection to the art of cigar-making, Blas embarked on his quest. He began small, working side by side with his employees, laboring tirelessly, perfecting the craft of blending tobacco leaves into cigars that were nothing short of exquisite. Rumors of the quality of his cigars spread like wildfire, and soon, his cigars became legends in their own right.

As the dream unfolds, I see Blas's factory transformed into a bustling hive of activity, a testament to his commitment to excellence. His loyal workforce mirrored his dedication, forging bonds that transcended the realm of employer and employee. They crafted each cigar with a sense of pride and artistry, each one bearing a badge of honor.

Blas's charisma extended beyond the factory walls. He became a pillar of the community, known not just for his business acumen, but for his boundless generosity. He poured his heart and resources into supporting community projects, schools, and charities, leaving an indelible mark on the town he had come to love. After touring the factory, Blas shows me his life full of social activities, especially the masonic lodge where he belonged, as well as his companionship with friends. His happiness is palpable, a symbol of the American Dream fulfilled. Unfortunately, it would not last. Surrounding his American dream shadows danced, and a sinister presence loomed. An organized crime gang from New Orleans had stretched the greedy fingers of its black hand into every corner of Ybor City, including its lucrative cigar industry. Their intent was clear: control everything, at any cost.

Two shadowy presences emerge from the mist, and the words, *soldiers of The Sicilian Black Hand,* resonated in my mind like a whispered curse. This New Orleans organized crime gang, like a creeping fog, had swiftly infiltrated the city, exploiting its vices and vulnerabilities.

But their intentions reached far beyond mere illicit activities, such as gambling and prostitution. Their greedy eyes were fixed upon the city's most precious jewel—the cigar industry. The factories, the very lifeblood of Ybor City, had drawn the mafia-like moths to a mesmerizing flame. Their ambition was ruthless, their goal clear: to seize control of the cigar business that thrived within the city's heart.

As the dream continues to unfold, I see two men dressed in suits approaching Blas with a proposition. They sought to buy his thriving cigar factory for a penance of its worth. Their offer was laced with coercion and threats of exposing his covert homosexual relationships. But Blas, a man of unwavering principles, would not yield. He clung to his life's work, his factory, and the livelihoods of his loyal employees. In this moment of refusal, battle lines were drawn, and the conflict escalated.

Tensions simmered, and in the dream's shifting landscape, I saw a black hand over Ybor City as it became a powder keg of uncertainty. The mafia grew bolder, resorting to intimidation and threats to bend the will of those who dared stand against them, including law enforcement officers.

As the pressure from the mafioso intensified, it fueled Blas's determination to protect not only his factory but also the livelihoods of the workers who depended on it. Each day, he stood resolute against the storm, refusing to yield to the threats and intimidation tactics employed by the gang's enforcers.

As the dream deepens, the sun casts long, eerie shadows over the factory floor. Blas Trujillos, the unyielding defender of his cigar empire and the hopes of his workers, sits in his office, oblivious to the sinister presence lurking nearby.

In a moment that sends shivers through me, the hitmen, sent by the criminal syndicate, emerge from the shadows. Their faces remain hidden, masked by darkness, as they approach Blas's office. Finally, the two of them enter and close the door. They exchanged words with Blas for a few seconds, seemingly offering him a last chance to sell his factory; then, the gunman drew a pistol from underneath his suit jacket and put a bullet into Blas's forehead at close range. The cold and calculating hitmen meticulously stage the crime scene. The two of them quickly pulled Blas out of his chair and laid him on the floor beside his desk. They placed the pistol used to kill him within an inch of his right hand. News of Blas Trujillo's demise ripples through Ybor City, and the community mourns the loss of a beloved leader and visionary.

At the heart of this disquieting gloom stands the Marshal—a figure entrusted with upholding the very laws that have crumbled under the weight of his fear of a darker force. He is a man of influence, but not one derived from the people he swore to protect. Instead, his actions emanate from a shadowy alliance with the criminal syndicate, a malevolent bond that has ensnared his soul through intimidation.

Afraid of retribution from the mafia, the Marshal acts swiftly in response to Bias Trujillo's murder. Despite mounting evidence that points to foul play, he hastily declares the death a suicide, avoiding a thorough investigation. His pronouncement sends shockwaves through Ybor City, leaving a cloud of suspicion hanging over the official account of events.

As the dream continues to unfold, I see his brothers, friends, and former employees, their doubts growing with each passing day. Their determination to uncover the truth becomes an unquenchable fire burning within them. Yet, they are confronted with a formidable obstacle in their quest for justice— a corrupt and fearful marshal, The marshal's role in this dark conspiracy becomes a focal point, a symbol of betrayal to the very ideals he was meant to uphold. The very person entrusted with maintaining law and order has become a fearful agent of deceit.

Blas shows me a scene where he is attending mass. I can feel his gratitude towards God for the wonderful life he's been given. I then see him in a freemason's apron participating in a ritual with other freemasons. As the dream fades, I hear him say:

> I did not kill myself. I was murdered. A man from the *Black Hand* killed me, and the marshal covered it up! I am a good soul and deserve to be in heaven! Please tell everyone that I was murdered, so my soul can rest.

My Psychic Impressions of Blas Trujillo

Both a practicing Catholic and a high-ranking Freemason, Mr. Trujillo was a man of faith and mysticism. He had many wonderful, loving friends and his business was prospering greatly. He was living the American dream. Although he held many secrets about his private life, he had no reason to kill himself. He had many lovers over the decades and broke many hearts, but none of his lovers wanted him dead. They just wanted his love and commitment which he was unable to give due to society's norms. I believe Mr. Trujillo came to me in a dream to set the record straight. He asked me to tell his story and reveal the truth so that he could finally have peace of mind and cross over. I made a promise to Mr. Trujillo to reveal his murderers by publishing his story. Although they appear to have gotten away with their crime in the physical realm, they are definitely paying for it in the afterlife. Word has it that they are in a cold and dark place!

~ 6 ~

CASE FILE # 5: JULIA WALLACE-THE WOLVERTON STREET MURDER OF 1931

Julia Wallace
Public Domain

Case Summary

Name of Deceased: Julia Wallace

Date of Birth: April 24, 1861

Date of Death: January 20, 1931

Location: 29 Wolverton Street, Liverpool, England

Deceased Found by: William Wallace

Relationship to the Deceased: Husband

Complainant: John Johnson notified the police at William Wallace's request.

Relationship to the Deceased: Neighbor

Witnesses: William Wallace, John Johnson, and Florence Johnson witnessed the crime scene. No one witnessed the murder.

Estimated Time of Death: Approximately between 1845 (6:45 pm) and 2045 (8:45 pm).

Position of Body: Julia was discovered lying on her right-hand side. Her legs were slightly parted with her feet lying flat on their sides close to the right-hand end of the fireplace. Her right arm was hidden beneath her body. Her left arm was bent at the elbow with the forearm resting over her chest, the fingers almost touching the floor.

Wounds: Visible brain matter oozed out of a large open wound in her skull.

Blood Splatters: Blood was sprayed as high as 7 feet off the floor, spattering the walls, furniture, various photographs, and Julia's framed paintings. The wall above the piano also received some of the blood spatter. A large pool of blood had also collected under her body with two other blood pools in a circle round to the front of the easy chair to the left of the fireplace.

Autopsy Findings: The autopsy findings as reported by Professor MacFall concluded that the cause of death was due to the fracture of the skull by someone striking the deceased three or four times with terrific force with a hard, large-headed instrument.

Disposition: Cold Case, Never Solved

Background Informant Source: Qualtrough, R.M., (2020, January 26). The Murder of Julia Wallace. The Julia Wallace Murder Foundation. https://www.williamherbertwallace.com/general/the-murder-of-julia-wallace/

Background on the Murder of Julia Wallace

On the evening of January 19, 1931, William Herbert Wallace, a middle-aged insurance agent, arrived at his home at 29 Wolverton Street, Liverpool, to find his wife, Julia, bludgeoned to death in the front parlor of their house. She had been brutally attacked with a blunt instrument, and her body was lying in a pool of blood.

William Wallace immediately contacted the police to report the murder. The investigation that followed was complex and puzzling. There was no clear motive for the murder, as the couple appeared to have a stable and uneventful marriage. Suspicion fell on Wallace himself, and he was arrested and charged with the murder.

The case against William Wallace relied heavily on circumstantial evidence. The prosecution argued that he had meticulously planned the murder to establish an alibi. Wallace had purportedly received a telephone call from a mysterious individual named *R. M. Qualtrough* who asked him to meet for a business opportunity at 25 Menlove Gardens East (a nonexistent address) at 7:30 pm the following evening. Wallace claimed he went to the meeting but found nothing there.

During the trial, Wallace's defense presented evidence that he couldn't have committed the murder due to the tight timeline and that the mysterious Qualtrough call was genuine. However, the evidence was not conclusive, and the jury found Wallace guilty. He was sentenced to death.

But the case took a dramatic turn when the Court of Criminal Appeal overturned Wallace's conviction, citing insufficient evidence and questionable police conduct. Wallace was released from prison after spending over a year behind bars. The case remains one of the most perplexing unsolved murders in British criminal history.

To this day, the identity of Julia Wallace's killer remains a mystery. The case has generated various theories and speculations, and it continues to capture the imagination of those interested in unsolved mysteries and true crime.

Julia Tells Her Story

Julia communicated her story to me in a vision. This vision played out like a movie in my head in full color with audio. I heard knocking coming from what I perceived to be the back door. I watched as Mrs. Wallace walked down a flight of stairs and through a dark room, which appeared to be a kitchen, to get to the door on the opposite side. She asked who the caller was, and I heard a man say in a hushed, gravelly tone of voice:

"Mrs. Wallace, it's Gordy, and I really need to talk to you. I hate to impose upon you, but I need some advice on how to make up with my girl. She's very upset with me."

Julia hastily opened the door, and said, "Of course, I'll be happy to help in any way that I can. Come on in and sit down at the table in the living kitchen."

In walked a young man wearing a nice, dark-colored, three-piece suit. He had a full head of dark hair and was well-shaven. He smiled as he hugged Mrs. Wallace. She walked over to a gaslight on the wall and lit it before walking over to the sink where she filled a tea pot with water. Then she walked over to a gas stove, placed the tea kettle on the grate, took a match from a shelf above the stove, and lit the burner.

Moving along in the vision, I saw her in the larger kitchen standing in front of what appeared to be a food preparation area, this could have been either a tabletop or countertop. As instructed, Gordy sat down at the table. I felt that Julia was well acquainted with this young man. In my mind's eye, I saw past images of him singing while she played the piano. Shortly after Gordy sat down at the table, Julia placed a cup of tea and a sandwich in front of him. She sat down with him while he hurriedly scuffed down his food. After he had eaten, they chatted for a little while longer. Then she suggested that they should retire to the living room and sing a few songs before the evening was over.

He smiled in agreement and I heard him say, “That’s a wonderful idea!”

Julia said, "Bravo, I’ll go prepare the living room."

I watched as she stood up and walked out of the room.

As soon as Julia left the room, Gordy quickly jumped up and ran over to a bookshelf where he took down a rectangular, metal box from the top shelf. He opened the lid, and without looking at the contents, grabbed a handful of money before returning the box to the shelf.

I see Julia entering a room through a door next to the door she had just exited from the living kitchen. Once in this room, she realized she had forgotten the matches needed to light the pilot on the gas fireplace. She turned around and walked back into the living kitchen just in time to catch Gordy returning the box to the shelf.

With a tone of shock and disbelief, she said, “Gordy! Are you taking money from the cash box? Are you robbing my husband after all he has done for you? Now, please put the money back. I can give you a loan from my own money if you need it!”

She walked over to a desk in the back of the room and took a box of matches out of a drawer. As she walked out the door on her way to the living room, she said, “Now hurry along. We have music to play.”

She made her way through the darkness of the living room to get to the fireplace on the left-hand side of the room. Over this fireplace was a mirror hanging on the wall. She bent over to ignite the pilot light and as she stood up, she caught the dark reflection of her attacker as he began assaulting her. He beat her repeatedly over the head with what looked like a metal pipe. Each blow he delivered was forceful and deliberate. As she tried to turn and run from her attacker, he struck the final blow, and she collapsed to the floor, blood gushing from her head wound.

Careful not to touch the walls, he ran upstairs and into the bathroom where he washed the blood off his hands and the tool he used to kill Julia. He shook his hands dry and then wiped them on his bloodied coat.

He ran back down the stairs, turned off the gas light in the living kitchen, and quickly ran out of the room and over to the back door of the cooking kitchen. He tugged at the door a time or two, and finally, it became unstuck and he opened it slowly just enough to glance outside. Once he made sure the coast was clear, he quickly scurried out, gently pulling the door behind him. I didn't hear the door shut, but I did hear a clicking sound when he closed it. I saw him move swiftly along a paved alleyway into the velvety darkness and cover of night.

My Psychic Impressions of Julia Wallace

I perceived that Mrs. Wallace was a kind and fun-loving person. She was the type of individual who would give you the shirt off her back if you needed it. Although Mr. Wallace was stoic and did not appear to be as kind or fun-loving as his wife, he did have a mild-mannered nature. He was very much, and still is, a gentle soul. He would have never plotted or implemented the murder of his wife. He enjoyed a low-key life.

I believe my vision, viewed through the eyes of Julia Wallace, reveals the true culprit—Richard Gordon Parry aka Gordy. The murderer is long dead and cannot be brought to justice on this side of the veil. Regardless, I hope publishing Julia's story will bring peace and closure for her.

The 1931 murder of Julia Wallace continues to captivate the imagination of true crime enthusiasts and amateur sleuths, as it raises questions about the adequacy of the investigation, the reliability of witnesses, and the possibility of a meticulously planned frame-up, possibly by Gordon Parry. Until now, it has remained an unsolved puzzle, shrouded in mystery and intrigue. I promised Julia that I would tell her story and reveal her murderer. I have kept my promise.

About the Author

Shirley Smolko, The Venetian Medium, is a gifted natural Psychic Medium, which means she was born with the ability to perceive psychic information and communicate with the souls of people who have passed away. In addition to being a Psychic Medium, Shirley is a publisher, author, and student. She holds a Bachelor of Science in Nursing, a Master of Business Administration, and a Master's in Accounting. She lives in the USA with her husband, Joe, and two cats, Zoey and Cecilia. To learn more about Shirley, her books, and her latest activities, visit venetianmedium.com or cavallaropub.com.

OTHER BOOKS BY SHIRLEY SMOLKO

My Adventures as a Psychic Nurse & Medium: Spirits Everywhere! (Previously published as: Adventures of a Psychic Nurse: Spirits Everywhere!)
My Adventures as a Psychic Nurse & Medium: Haunted Hospital! (Previously published as: More Adventures of a Psychic Nurse: Haunted Hospitals!)
Just a Thought Away: Communicating With Loved Ones In Spirit
Money Wants Me!
Money at Your Command!
Secret to the Science of Getting Rich
At Your Command!
Revelations of the Afterlife: A New Arrival
Wisdom From the Wealthy Dead: A Medium Interviews the Souls of Three American Tycoons
Wisdom From the Wealthy Dead: A Medium Interviews the Soul of Andrew Carnegie
The Murdered Dead Speak: Book I
Be Sure to Look for Even More Books to Come!"

www.ingramcontent.com/pod-product-compliance
Lightning Source LLC
Chambersburg PA
CBHW070127030426
42335CB00016B/2293

* 9 7 8 1 9 5 8 1 0 4 0 9 5 *